JOHN
MACARTHUR

2 CORINTHIANS

~ *Words from a Caring Shepherd* ~

NELSON IMPACT
A Division of Thomas Nelson Publishers
Since 1798

www.thomasnelson.com

2 Corinthians
MacArthur Bible Studies

Copyright © 2007, John MacArthur.

Published by Nelson Impact, a Division of Thomas Nelson, Inc., P.O. Box 141000, Nashville, Tennessee 37214.

Produced with the assistance of the Livingstone Corporation. Project staff include Jake Barton, Mary Horner Collins, and Andy Culbertson.

Project editor: Len Woods

Cover Art by Kirk Luttrell, Livingstone Corporation

Interior Design and Composition by Joel Bartlett, Livingstone Corporation

ISBN-10: 1-4185-0962-0
ISBN-13: 978-1-4185-0962-0

Printed in the United States of America.
07 08 09 RRD 9 8 7 6 5 4 3 2 1

CONTENTS

Introduction to 2 Corinthians

This is the second New Testament epistle the apostle Paul wrote to the Christians in the city of Corinth.

Author and Date

That the apostle Paul wrote 2 Corinthians is uncontested; the lack of any motive for a forger to write this highly personal, biographical epistle has led even the most critical scholars to affirm Paul as its author.

Several considerations establish a feasible date for the writing of this letter. Extrabiblical sources indicate that July, AD 51 is the most likely date for the beginning of Gallio's proconsulship (see Acts 18:12). Paul's trial before him at Corinth (Acts 18:12–17) probably took place shortly after Gallio assumed office. Leaving Corinth (probably in AD 52), Paul sailed for Palestine (Acts 18:18), thus concluding his second missionary journey. Returning to Ephesus on his third missionary journey (probably in AD 52), Paul ministered there for about two and a half years (Acts 19:8, 10). The apostle wrote 1 Corinthians from Ephesus toward the close of that period (1 Cor. 16:8), most likely in AD 55. Since Paul planned to stay in Ephesus until the following spring, and 2 Corinthians was written after he left Ephesus, the most likely date for 2 Corinthians is late AD 55 or very early AD 56.

Background and Setting

Paul's association with the important commercial city of Corinth began on his second missionary journey (Acts 18:1–18), when he spent eighteen months ministering there. After leaving Corinth, Paul heard of immorality in the Corinthian church and wrote a letter (that has since been lost) to confront that sin, referred to in 1 Corinthians 5:9. During his ministry in Ephesus, he received further reports of trouble in the Corinthian church in the form of divisions among them (1 Cor. 1:11). In addition, the Corinthians wrote Paul a letter (1 Cor. 7:1) asking for clarification of some issues. Paul responded by writing the letter known as 1 Corinthians. Planning to remain at Ephesus a little longer (1 Cor. 16:8, 9), Paul sent Timothy to Corinth (1 Cor. 4:17; 16:10–11). Disturbing news reached the apostle (possibly from Timothy) of further difficulties at Corinth, including the arrival of false, self-styled apostles (11:13).

To create the platform to teach their false gospel, they began by assaulting the character of Paul. They had to convince the people to turn from Paul to them if they were to succeed in preaching demon doctrine. Temporarily abandoning the work at Ephesus, Paul went immediately to Corinth. The visit (known as the "painful visit," 2:1) was not a successful one from Paul's perspective; someone in the Corinthian church (possibly one of the false apostles) even openly insulted him (2:5–8, 10; 7:12). Saddened by the Corinthians' lack of loyalty to defend him, seeking to spare them further reproof (see 1:23), and perhaps hoping time would bring them to their senses, Paul returned to Ephesus. From Ephesus, Paul wrote what is known as the "severe letter" (2:4) and sent it with Titus to Corinth (7:5–16). Leaving Ephesus after the riot sparked by Demetrius (Acts 19:23–20:1), Paul went to Troas to meet Titus (2:12–13). But Paul was so anxious for news of how the Corinthians had responded to the "severe letter" that he could not minister there though the Lord had opened the door (2:12; see 7:5). So he left for Macedonia to look for Titus (2:13). To Paul's immense relief and joy, Titus met him with the news that the majority of the Corinthians had repented of their rebellion against Paul (7:7). Wise enough to know that some rebellious attitudes still smoldered under the surface and could erupt again, Paul wrote (possibly from Philippi, see 11:9 with Phil. 4:15; also, some early manuscripts list Philippi as the place of writing) the Corinthians the letter called 2 Corinthians.

In this letter, though the apostle expresses his relief and joy at their repentance (7:8–16), his main concern is to defend his apostleship (chs. 1–7), exhort the Corinthians to resume preparations for the collection for the poor at Jerusalem (chs. 8, 9), and confront the false apostles head-on (chs. 10–13). He then went to Corinth, as he had written (12:14; 13:1–2). The Corinthians' participation in the Jerusalem offering (Rom. 15:26) implies that Paul's third visit to that church was successful.

Historical and Theological Themes

Second Corinthians complements the historical record of Paul's dealings with the Corinthian church recorded in Acts and 1 Corinthians. It also contains important biographical data on Paul throughout.

Although an intensely personal letter, written by the apostle in the heat of battle against those attacking his credibility, 2 Corinthians contains several important theological themes. It portrays God the Father as a merciful comforter (1:3; 7:6), the Creator (4:6), and the One who raised Jesus from the dead (4:14; see 13:4), and will raise believers as well (1:9). Jesus Christ is the One who suffered (1:5), who fulfilled God's promises (1:20), who was the proclaimed Lord (4:5), who manifested God's glory (4:6), and who became poor for believers (8:9; see Phil. 2:5–8). The letter portrays the Holy Spirit as God (3:17, 18) and the guarantee of believers' salvation (1:22; 5:5). Satan is identified as the "god of this age" (4:4; see 1 John 5:19), a deceiver (11:14), and the leader of human and angelic deceivers (11:15). The end times include both the believer's glorification (4:16–5:8) and his or her judgment (5:10). The glorious truth of God's sovereignty in salvation is the theme of 5:14–21, while 7:9–10 sets forth man's response to God's offer of salvation—genuine repentance. Second Corinthians also presents the clearest, most concise summary of the substitutionary atonement of Christ to be found anywhere in Scripture (5:21; see Isa. 53) and defines the mission of the church to proclaim reconciliation (5:18–20). Finally, the nature of the new covenant receives its fullest exposition outside the book of Hebrews (3:6–16).

INTERPRETIVE CHALLENGES

The main challenge confronting the interpreter is the relationship of chapters 10–13 to chapters 1–9. The identity of Paul's opponents at Corinth has produced various interpretations, as has the identity of the brother who accompanied Titus to Corinth (8:18, 22). It is also uncertain whether the offender mentioned in 2:5–8 is the incestuous man of 1 Corinthians 5. It is difficult to explain Paul's vision (12:1–5) and to identify specifically his "thorn in the flesh," the "messenger of Satan [sent] to buffet [him]" (12:7). These and other interpretive problems will be dealt with in the notes on the appropriate passages.

Notes

SUFFERING

2 Corinthians 1:1–11

DRAWING NEAR

Think of a time when you were hurting emotionally or struggling with difficulties. What did friends do (or not do) that brought you the most comfort?

_____

_____

_____

_____

_____

_____

_____

THE CONTEXT

The major theme in this epistle is Paul's defense of his apostleship against the many attacks of the false teachers in Corinth. In the opening section of 2 Corinthians, Paul defends himself against the false charge that his trials were God's punishment for his sin and unfaithfulness. The apostle makes the point that God was comforting him in his suffering, not chastening him. In so doing, he penned one of the most significant passages on comfort anywhere in Scripture.

KEYS TO THE TEXT

Tribulation: When talking about troubles and tribulations, Paul used the Greek word that means "pressure." Throughout all the pressures, stress, persecution, and trials, Paul experienced God's comforting, strengthening presence. The apostle's life was thus an amazing juxtaposition of affliction and comfort, a seeming paradox he expressed later in this letter (see 4:7–11). Because God constantly comforted and protected him, Paul was indestructible until the time came in God's sovereign plan for him to die.

5

UNLEASHING THE TEXT

Read 1:1–11, noting the key words and definitions next to the passage.

2 Corinthians 1:1–11 (NKJV)

apostle (v. 1)—This refers to Paul's official position as a messenger sent by Christ.

by the will of God (v. 1)—Paul was saying his mission was not a self-appointed one, or based on his own achievements; rather, his credentials were by divine appointment, and his letter reflected not his own message, but the words of Christ.

Timothy *our* brother (v. 1)—Paul's cherished son in the faith and a dominant person in Paul's life and ministry, who was with Paul during the founding of the church in Corinth (Acts 18:1–5)

Grace . . . peace (v. 2)—This was part of Paul's normal salutation in his letters. "Grace" is God's unmerited favor, and "peace" one of its benefits.

God and Father of our Lord Jesus Christ (v. 3)—Paul praised the true God who revealed Himself in His Son, who is of the same essence with the Father; He is the anointed one (Christ) and sovereign (Lord) and Redeemer (Jesus).

1 *Paul, an apostle of Jesus Christ by the will of God, and Timothy our brother, to the church of God which is at Corinth, with all the saints who are in all Achaia:*

2 *Grace to you and peace from God our Father and the Lord Jesus Christ.*

3 *Blessed be the God and Father of our Lord Jesus Christ, the Father of mercies and God of all comfort,*

4 *who comforts us in all our tribulation, that we may be able to comfort those who are in any trouble, with the comfort with which we ourselves are comforted by God.*

5 *For as the sufferings of Christ abound in us, so our consolation also abounds through Christ.*

6 *Now if we are afflicted, it is for your consolation and salvation, which is effective for enduring the same sufferings which we also suffer. Or if we are comforted, it is for your consolation and salvation.*

Father of mercies (v. 3)—Paul borrowed from Jewish liturgical language and a synagogue prayer that called for God to treat the sinful individual with kindness, love, and tenderness.

God of all comfort (v. 3)—An Old Testament description of God (see Isa. 40:1; 51:3, 12; 66:13), who is the ultimate source of every true act of comfort. The Greek word for "comfort" is related to the familiar word *paraclete*, "one who comes alongside to help," another name for the Holy Spirit (see John 14:26; Phil. 2:1). "Comfort" often connotes softness and ease, but that is not its meaning here. Paul was saying that God came to him in the middle of his sufferings and troubles to strengthen him and give him courage and boldness (see vv. 4–10).

tribulation (v. 4)—This term refers to crushing pressure, because in Paul's life and ministry there was always something attempting to weaken him, restrict or confine his ministry, or even crush out his life.

that we may be able to comfort (v. 4)—Comfort from God is not an end in itself. Its purpose is that believers also might be comforters.

sufferings of Christ abound (v. 5)—God's comfort to believers extends to the boundaries of their suffering for Christ. The more they endure righteous suffering, the greater will be their comfort and reward.

consolation (v. 6)—comfort

salvation (v. 6)—This refers to the Corinthians' ongoing perseverance to final, completed salvation, when they will be glorified.

7 *And our hope for you is steadfast, because we know that as you are partakers of the sufferings, so also you will partake of the consolation.*

8 *For we do not want you to be ignorant, brethren, of our trouble which came to us in Asia: that we were burdened beyond measure, above strength, so that we despaired even of life.*

9 *Yes, we had the sentence of death in ourselves, that we should not trust in ourselves but in God who raises the dead,*

10 *who delivered us from so great a death, and does deliver us; in whom we trust that He will still deliver us,*

11 *you also helping together in prayer for us, that thanks may be given by many persons on our behalf for the gift granted to us through many.*

partakers of the sufferings (v. 7)—Some in the church at Corinth, perhaps the majority, were suffering for righteousness, as Paul was.

our (v. 8)—an editorial plural, which Paul used throughout the letter; usually a humble reference to Paul himself, but in this instance it could include others as well

trouble which came to us in Asia (v. 8)—The details of this situation are not known.

despaired even of life (v. 8)—The Greek word for "despaired" literally means "no passage," the total absence of an exit (see 2 Tim. 4:6). Paul faced something that was beyond human survival and was extremely discouraging because he believed it threatened to end his ministry prematurely.

the sentence of death (v. 9)—The word for "sentence" is a technical term that indicated the passing of an official resolution, in this case the death sentence. Paul was so absolutely sure he was going to die for the gospel that he pronounced the death sentence upon himself.

who raises the dead (v. 9)—A Jewish descriptive term for God, used in synagogue worship language. Paul understood that trust in God's power to raise the dead was the only hope of rescue from his extreme circumstances.

helping together in prayer (v. 11)—Intercessory prayer is crucial to the expression of God's power and sovereign purpose.

thanks may be given (v. 11)—Prayer's duty is not to change God's plans, but to give thanks for them and glorify Him.

the gift (v. 11)—probably better translated "favor" or "blessing," as in God's undeserved favor or the divine answer to prayer Paul would receive in being delivered from death

1) Who are the senders and who are the recipients of this letter?

_____

_____

_____

2) How does Paul describe God in the opening sentences of this epistle?

_____

_____

_____

3) List the various words and phrases Paul uses to describe his dire situation.

_____

_____

4) What "positive" results can come from times of suffering?

_____

_____

_____

5) What is the role of prayer during hard times?

_____

_____

_____

_____

GOING DEEPER

To get another perspective on suffering and God's comfort, read Romans 8:31–37.

31 *What then shall we say to these things? If God is for us, who can be against us?*

32 *He who did not spare His own Son, but delivered Him up for us all, how shall He not with Him also freely give us all things?*

33 *Who shall bring a charge against God's elect? It is God who justifies.*

34 *Who is he who condemns? It is Christ who died, and furthermore is also risen, who is even at the right hand of God, who also makes intercession for us.*

35 *Who shall separate us from the love of Christ? Shall tribulation, or distress, or persecution, or famine, or nakedness, or peril, or sword?*

36 *As it is written: "For Your sake we are killed all day long; we are accounted as sheep for the slaughter."*

37 *Yet in all these things we are more than conquerors through Him who loved us.*

Exploring the Meaning

6) What is the primary lesson or spiritual truth found in Romans 8:31–38?

_____

_____

_____

_____

_____

7) Paul says the hardships he endured were the sufferings of Christ. In what way?

_____

_____

_____

8) How would you answer a new believer who inquired, "Why does God allow His most devoted servants to suffer? It seems like He would shield them from such trouble."

_____

_____

_____

_____

_____

9) Paul models an attitude of praise (v. 3) and thankfulness (v. 11). How can a Christian develop this character trait, despite his or her circumstances?

_____

_____

_____

_____

TRUTH FOR TODAY

A believer's spiritual maturity can be measured by what it takes to steal his joy. Joy is a fruit of a Spirit-controlled life (Gal. 5:22). We are to rejoice always. In all circumstances the Holy Spirit produces joy, so there ought not to be any time when we are not rejoicing in some way. Change, confusion, trials, attacks, unmet desires, conflict, and strained relationships can throw us off balance and rob us of our joy if we're not careful. It's then we should cry out like the psalmist, "Restore to me the joy of Your salvation" (Ps. 51:12 NKJV). Jesus said, "In the world you will have tribulation; but be of good cheer, I have overcome the world" (John 16:33 NKJV); and James said, "Count it all joy when you fall into various trials" (James 1:2 NKJV). God has His own profound purpose in our afflictions, but He never takes away our joy. To maintain our joy we must adopt God's perspective regarding our trials. When we yield to the working of His Spirit in our lives, our difficulties will not overwhelm us.

REFLECTING ON THE TEXT

10) What hardships or trials are you currently experiencing? Learning from Paul's example, how can you develop a new perspective on suffering?

---

11) Think back over your life, especially over the darkest times. List the positive things that God has brought out of those situations.

---

12) In another epistle Paul wrote, "In everything give thanks" (1 Thess. 5:18 NKJV). Take a few minutes to express your gratitude to God for ten specific things in your life.

_____

_____

_____

_____

_____

_____

_____

_____

Personal Response

Write out additional reflections, questions you may have, or a prayer.

_____

_____

_____

_____

_____

_____

_____

_____

_____

_____

ADDITIONAL NOTES

PAUL'S MINISTRY PLANS

DRAWING NEAR

In his desire to spread the gospel, Paul made many plans, but God often changed them. When was the last time you made specific plans only to have them change in ways you never anticipated?

_____

_____

_____

How did you see God's hand in that circumstance, or in other unplanned events of your life?

_____

_____

_____

_____

THE CONTEXT

The letter of 2 Corinthians is Paul's defense of his ministry against slanderous attacks. In chapter 1, he gives a general defense of his personal integrity. He replies to the specific charge that he was not trustworthy. Because Paul had made a change in his travel plans, his opponents charged him with being dishonest, unfaithful, fickle, and vacillating. But rather than engage in a battle of "he said/they said," Paul elevated the whole discussion to the motives and attitudes of his heart. By so doing, he provides a priceless look at a noble man of God.

Then he shifted gears, urging the Corinthians to forgive a man who had apparently assaulted Paul (verbally and publicly) during the apostle's "painful visit." Following Paul's prior instructions, the Corinthian church had disciplined this member, putting him out of the fellowship. Because the man eventually repented, Paul forgave him, and he instructed the Corinthians to do likewise.

13

Keys to the Text

Conscience: This word in the Greek conveys the idea of the soul reflecting on itself or knowing oneself. Even those without God's written law have an innate moral sense of right and wrong. The conscience either affirms right behavior or condemns sinful behavior. It is not infallible, however, as it holds people only to their highest perceived standard. Thus believers need to set that standard to the highest possible level by submitting to God's Word. As they continually fill their minds with the truths of Scripture, their consciences will then call them to live according to that law.

Unleashing the Text

Read 1:12–2:13, noting the key words and definitions next to the passage.

boasting (v. 12)—Paul often used this word, and it can also be rendered "proud confidence." Used negatively, it refers to unwarranted bragging about one's own merits and achievements; but Paul used it positively to denote legitimate confidence in what God had done in his life.

conscience (v. 12)—The soul's warning system allows human beings to contemplate their motives and actions and make moral evaluations of what is right and wrong. Paul's fully enlightened conscience exonerated him completely.

fleshly wisdom (v. 12)—wisdom that is based on worldly, human insight

in part (v. 14)—As the Corinthians read and heard Paul's unfolding instruction to them, they continued to understand more.

2 Corinthians 1:12–2:13 (NKJV)

12 *For our boasting is this: the testimony of our conscience that we conducted ourselves in the world in simplicity and godly sincerity, not with fleshly wisdom but by the grace of God, and more abundantly toward you.*

13 *For we are not writing any other things to you than what you read or understand. Now I trust you will understand, even to the end*

14 *(as also you have understood us in part), that we are your boast as you also are ours, in the day of the Lord Jesus.*

15 *And in this confidence I intended to come to you before, that you might have a second benefit—*

16 *to pass by way of you to Macedonia, to come again from Macedonia to you, and be helped by you on my way to Judea.*

we are your boast (v. 14)—more clearly translated, "we are your reason to be proud"

the day of the Lord Jesus (v. 14)—Paul eagerly longed for the Lord's coming, when they would rejoice over each other in glory.

a second benefit (v. 15)—Or, "twice receive a blessing." Paul's original plan was to visit the Corinthians twice so that they might receive a double blessing.

come again (v. 16)—Paul had planned to leave Ephesus, stop at Corinth on the way to Macedonia, and return to Corinth again after his ministry in Macedonia (see 1 Cor. 16:5–7). For some reason, Paul was unable to stop in Corinth the first time, and the false apostles seized upon that honest change of schedule and tried to use it to discredit Paul as untrustworthy.

17 Therefore, when I was planning this, did I do it lightly? Or the things I plan, do I plan according to the flesh, that with me there should be Yes, Yes, and No, No?

18 But as God is faithful, our word to you was not Yes and No.

19 For the Son of God, Jesus Christ, who was preached among you by us—by me, Silvanus, and Timothy—was not Yes and No, but in Him was Yes.

20 For all the promises of God in Him are Yes, and in Him Amen, to the glory of God through us.

21 Now He who establishes us with you in Christ and has anointed us is God,

22 who also has sealed us and given us the Spirit in our hearts as a guarantee.

23 Moreover I call God as witness against my soul, that to spare you I came no more to Corinth.

24 Not that we have dominion over your faith, but are fellow workers for your joy; for by faith you stand.

2:1 But I determined this within myself, that I would not come again to you in sorrow.

2 For if I make you sorrowful, then who is he who makes me glad but the one who is made sorrowful by me?

3 And I wrote this very thing to you, lest, when I came, I should have sorrow over those from whom I ought to have joy, having confidence in you all that my joy is the joy of you all.

4 For out of much affliction and anguish of heart I wrote to you, with many tears, not that you should be grieved, but that you might know the love which I have so abundantly for you.

according to the flesh (v. 17)—Purely from a human viewpoint, apart from the leading of the Holy Spirit, this is someone who is unregenerate.

as God is faithful (v. 18)—Paul may have been making an oath and calling God to give testimony; whatever the case, he refers to God's trustworthiness and the fact that he represented Him as an honest spokesman.

not Yes and No (v. 18)—He was not saying "yes" and meaning "no." There was no duplicity with Paul.

Silvanus (v. 19)—the Latin name for Silas, Paul's companion on his second missionary journey (Acts 16–18) and fellow preacher at Corinth

Amen (v. 20)—The Hebrew word of affirmation (see Matt. 5:18; John 3:3; Rom. 1:25). Paul reminded them that they had said a collective "yes" to the truth of his preaching and teaching.

Christ . . . God . . . Spirit (vss. 21–22)—a clear reference to the three members of the Trinity

anointed (v. 21)—This word is borrowed from a commissioning service that would symbolically set apart kings, prophets, priests, and special servants. The Holy Spirit sets apart believers and empowers them for the service of gospel proclamation and ministry.

sealed us (v. 22)—refers to the ancient practice of placing soft wax on a document and imprinting the wax with a stamp that indicated authorship or ownership, authenticity, and protection

guarantee (v. 22)—A pledge or down payment. The Spirit is the down payment on the believer's eternal inheritance.

to spare you (v. 23)—Paul finally explained why he said he was coming, but did not. He did not come earlier because he wanted them to have time to repent of and correct their sinful behavior.

come again . . . in sorrow (2:1)—Paul, who had already had a painful confrontation at Corinth, was not eager to have another one.

if anyone has caused grief (v. 5)—The Greek construction of this clause assumes the condition to be true—Paul is acknowledging the reality of the offense and its ongoing effect, not on him, but on the church.

punishment ... inflicted by the majority (v. 6)—This indicates that the church in Corinth had followed the biblical process in disciplining the sinning man (see Matt. 18:15–20).

to forgive (v. 7)—It was time to grant forgiveness so the man's joy would be restored.

in the presence of Christ (v. 10)—Paul was constantly aware that his entire life was lived in the sight of God, who knew everything he thought, did, and said.

5 But if anyone has caused grief, he has not grieved me, but all of you to some extent—not to be too severe.

6 This punishment which was inflicted by the majority is sufficient for such a man,

7 so that, on the contrary, you ought rather to forgive and comfort him, lest perhaps such a one be swallowed up with too much sorrow.

8 Therefore I urge you to reaffirm your love to him.

9 For to this end I also wrote, that I might put you to the test, whether you are obedient in all things.

10 Now whom you forgive anything, I also forgive. For if indeed I have forgiven anything, I have forgiven that one for your sakes in the presence of Christ,

11 lest Satan should take advantage of us; for we are not ignorant of his devices.

devices (v. 11)—Wanting to produce sin and animosity that will destroy church unity, the devil uses every possible approach to accomplish this—from legalism to libertinism, intolerance to excessive tolerance.

1) Paul defends himself in this letter. Why? What does Paul say about his conscience (1:12)?

_____

_____

_____

_____

_____

2) What were Paul's original plans where the Corinthians were concerned? What happened?

_____

_____

_____

_____

_____

3) What evidence does Paul cite in this passage to demonstrate his deep love for the Corinthians?

_____

_____

_____

4) Some Christians imagine that the apostle Paul was driven and task-oriented, steam-rolling over people's needs and feelings in order to "reach the world." Read back through the passage with a view to seeing Paul's character, his heart. What do you see?

_____

_____

_____

_____

5) In 2:5–11, Paul raises the issue of forgiveness. What is the situation here? What are Paul's instructions?

_____

_____

_____

_____

GOING DEEPER

Take a few minutes to gain more insight into Paul's character by reading 1 Corinthians 4:1–5.

1 *Let a man so consider us, as servants of Christ and stewards of the mysteries of God.*

2 *Moreover it is required in stewards that one be found faithful.*

3 *But with me it is a very small thing that I should be judged by you or by a human court. In fact, I do not even judge myself.*

4 *For I know of nothing against myself, yet I am not justified by this; but He who judges me is the Lord.*

5 *Therefore judge nothing before the time, until the Lord comes, who will both bring to light the hidden things of darkness and reveal the counsels of the hearts. Then each one's praise will come from God.*

Exploring the Meaning

6) Why does this passage suggest that our consciences ("counsels of the hearts"), while helpful, are not *fully* reliable?

7) What great promises do we find in 2 Corinthians 1:21–22? What are the implications of these truths for our daily lives?

8) The false teachers in Corinth had effectively spread the notion that Paul was fickle, unreliable, and selfish. People too lazy to investigate the truth believed these lies. What are the criteria you use for evaluating whether something or someone (a new product, a political candidate, a church, a biblical message) is what it purports to be?

9) How can Satan use an unforgiving spirit among Christians to wreak havoc in the church? Have you seen examples of this? Explain.

Truth for Today

The price of refusing to forgive is high. Unforgiveness produces hatred, bitterness, animosity, anger, and retribution. It not only clogs up the arteries but also the courts with thousands of vengeful lawsuits. Refusing to forgive imprisons people in their past. Unforgiving people keep their pain alive by constantly picking at the open wound and keeping it from healing. Bitterness takes root in their hearts and defiles them (Heb. 12:15). Anger rages out of control, and negative emotions run unchecked. Life is filled with turmoil and strife instead of joy and peace. On the other hand, forgiveness frees people from the past. It is liberating, exhilarating, and healthy. Forgiveness relieves tension, brings peace and joy, and restores relationships.

Reflecting on the Text

10) Paul's conscience was clear. He was not aware of any specific instance in which he had acted inappropriately toward the Corinthians. Can you make a similar claim with regard to the people in your life (family members, friends, neighbors, coworkers)? Is there anyone from whom you need to solicit forgiveness today?

_____

_____

_____

11) Paul was concerned about the Corinthians' spiritual health. Are there people in your life who might need to be encouraged or challenged spiritually? Pray for God's wisdom and courage to know how to proceed.

_____

_____

_____

_____

_____

_____

_____

PERSONAL RESPONSE

Write out additional reflections, questions you may have, or a prayer.

3

THE GLORY OF THE
NEW COVENANT

DRAWING NEAR

When you hear the term "new covenant," what comes to mind?

_____

_____

_____

_____

Think about the spiritual benefits of knowing Christ. How has He made you a new person?

_____

_____

_____

_____

_____

THE CONTEXT

Despite all their blind spots and failings, Paul loved the Corinthian church deeply. After all, he had invested at least eighteen months of his life ministering to them (see Acts 18:11). As we all know by experience, when we love others deeply, we open ourselves up to the possibility of deep hurt. And the Corinthians did wound Paul's heart by seriously entertaining the foolish teachings and outrageous accusations of his envious opponents.

In these verses Paul admitted his discouragement over the Corinthians' suspicions toward him. But then he also declared the encouragement he found in Christ. Paul then turned his thoughts and his pen toward the glorious issue of the "new covenant" relationship we can have with God. In this passage we find a brief summary of the characteristics of the complete salvation brought to us by Christ.

Keys to the Text

Fragrance of Christ: The imagery comes from the strong, sweet smell of incense from censers in the Roman Triumph parades; which, along with the fragrance of crushed flowers strewn under horses' hooves, produced a powerful aroma that filled the city. Paul was grateful for the privilege of being used as an influence for Christ (see Rom. 10:14–15) wherever he went.

Old and New Covenants: The word *covenant* is from the Greek word *diathēkē*, a general term for a binding agreement, sometimes translated "testament." A covenant always involves two or more specific parties, although the terms may be stipulated and fulfilled by only one. In the Old Testament the term is consistently used of God's covenants with His people—covenants that God alone initiated and established and that sometimes were conditional and sometimes not. The "old covenant" of law was given through Moses at Mount Sinai and required God's chosen people, the Jews, to keep all the commands He gave in conjunction with that covenant. The "new covenant" was made through Jesus' death and resurrection, and is a covenant of salvation by faith and grace.

Unleashing the Text

Read 2:12–3:18, noting the key words and definitions next to the passage.

2 Corinthians 2:12–3:18 (NKJV)

when I came to Troas (v. 12)—"Troas" was a seaport city north of Ephesus in the western Asia Minor province of Mysia (see Acts 16:7).

a door was opened to me (v. 12)—God sovereignly provided a great evangelistic opportunity for Paul, which may have led to the planting of the church in Troas (see Acts 20:5–12).

I had no rest in my spirit (v. 13)—Paul's concern for the

12 *Furthermore, when I came to Troas to preach Christ's gospel, and a door was opened to me by the Lord,*

13 *I had no rest in my spirit, because I did not find Titus my brother; but taking my leave of them, I departed for Macedonia.*

14 *Now thanks be to God who always leads us in triumph in Christ, and through us diffuses the fragrance of His knowledge in every place.*

problems in the Corinthian church and how its members were responding to both those problems and his instructions caused Paul debilitating restlessness and anxiety.

Titus (v. 13)—one of Paul's most important Gentile converts and closest associates in ministry

Macedonia (v. 13)—a province that bordered the northwest shore of the Aegean Sea, north of Achaia

Now thanks be to God (v. 14)—Paul turned from the difficulties of ministry, and by focusing on the privileges of his position in Christ, he regained his joyful perspective.

leads us in triumph in Christ (v. 14)—Paul drew from the imagery of the official and exalted Roman ceremony called the Triumph, in which a victorious general was honored with a festive, ceremonial parade through the streets of Rome.

15 For we are to God the fragrance of Christ among those who are being saved and among those who are perishing.

16 To the one we are the aroma of death leading to death, and to the other the aroma of life leading to life. And who is sufficient for these things?

17 For we are not, as so many, peddling the word of God; but as of sincerity, but as from God, we speak in the sight of God in Christ.

3:1 Do we begin again to commend ourselves? Or do we need, as some others, epistles of commendation to you or letters of commendation from you?

2 You are our epistle written in our hearts, known and read by all men;

3 clearly you are an epistle of Christ, ministered by us, written not with ink but by the Spirit of the living God, not on tablets of stone but on tablets of flesh, that is, of the heart.

4 And we have such trust through Christ toward God.

5 Not that we are sufficient of ourselves to think of anything as being from ourselves, but our sufficiency is from God,

6 who also made us sufficient as ministers of the new covenant, not of the letter but of the Spirit; for the letter kills, but the Spirit gives life.

the aroma of death . . . life (v. 16)—Paul used the style of Hebrew superlatives to emphasize the twofold effect of gospel preaching. To some, the message brings eternal life and ultimate glorification. To others, it is a stumbling stone of offense that brings eternal death (see 1 Pet. 2:6–8).

Do we begin again to commend ourselves? (3:1)—The Greek word for "commend" means "to introduce." Thus Paul was asking the Corinthians if he needed to reintroduce himself, as if they had never met, and prove himself once more. The form of the question demanded a negative answer.

letters of commendation (v. 1)—The false teachers also accused Paul of not possessing the appropriate documents to prove his legitimacy. Such letters were often used to introduce and authenticate someone to the first-century churches (see 1 Cor. 16:3, 10–11).

known and read by all men (v. 2)—The transformed lives of the Corinthians, that could be seen by all men, were Paul's most eloquent testimonial, better than any secondhand letter.

epistle of Christ (v. 3)—The false teachers did not have a letter of commendation signed by Christ, but Paul had the Corinthian believers' changed lives as proof that Christ had transformed them.

tablets of stone (v. 3)—a reference to the Ten Commandments

tablets of flesh . . . of the heart (v. 3)—More than just writing His law on stone, God was writing His law on the hearts of those people He transformed.

to think of anything (v. 5)—The Greek word for "think" can also mean "to consider" or "to reason." Paul disdained his own ability to reason, judge, or assess truth. Left to his own abilities, he was useless. He was dependent on divine revelation and the Holy Spirit's power.

new covenant (v. 6)—the covenant that provides forgiveness of sins through the death of Christ

the letter (v. 6)—a shallow, external conformity to the Law that missed its most basic requirement of holy and perfect love for God and man (Matt. 22:34–40) and distorted its true intention, which was to make a person recognize his sinfulness (see Rom. 2:27–29)

the letter kills, but the Spirit gives life (v. 6)—The letter kills in two ways: (1) It results in a living death. Before Paul was converted, he thought he was saved by keeping the Law, but all it did was kill his peace, joy, and hope. And (2) it results in spiritual death. His inability to truly keep the Law sentenced him to an eternal death.

the ministry of death (v. 7)— The Law is a killer in the sense that it brings knowledge of sin. It acts as a ministry of death because no one can satisfy its demands on his own and is therefore condemned.

was glorious (v. 7)—When God gave Moses the Law, His glory appeared on the mountain (Ex. 19:10–25; 20:18–26). Paul was not depreciating the Law; he was acknowledging that it was glorious because it reflected God's nature, will, and character.

could not look steadily at the face of Moses (v. 7)—The Israelites could not stare at Moses' face for too long because the reflective glory of God was too bright for them.

the glory of his countenance (v. 7)—When God manifested Himself, He did so by reducing His attributes to visible light.

ministry of the Spirit . . . exceeds much more in glory (vv. 8–9)—Paul is arguing that if such glory attended the giving of the Law under the ministry that brought death, how much more glorious will be the ministry of the Spirit in the new covenant which brings righteousness.

7 *But if the ministry of death, written and engraved on stones, was glorious, so that the children of Israel could not look steadily at the face of Moses because of the glory of his countenance, which glory was passing away,*

8 *how will the ministry of the Spirit not be more glorious?*

9 *For if the ministry of condemnation had glory, the ministry of righteousness exceeds much more in glory.*

10 *For even what was made glorious had no glory in this respect, because of the glory that excels.*

11 *For if what is passing away was glorious, what remains is much more glorious.*

12 *Therefore, since we have such hope, we use great boldness of speech—*

13 *unlike Moses, who put a veil over his face so that the children of Israel could not look steadily at the end of what was passing away.*

14 *But their minds were blinded. For until this day the same veil remains unlifted in the reading of the Old Testament, because the veil is taken away in Christ.*

15 *But even to this day, when Moses is read, a veil lies on their heart.*

16 *Nevertheless when one turns to the Lord, the veil is taken away.*

ministry of righteousness (v. 9)—the new covenant

what is passing away (v. 11)—The Law had a fading glory (see v. 7). It was not the final solution or the last word on the plight of sinners.

boldness of speech (v. 12)—The Greek word for "boldness" means "courageously." Because of his confidence, Paul preached the new covenant fearlessly, without any hesitation or timidity.

Moses, who put a veil over his face (v. 13)—The old covenant was veiled. It was shadowy. It was made up of types, pictures, symbols, and mystery. Moses communicated the glory of the old covenant with a certain obscurity.

the same veil remains . . . a veil lies on their heart (vv. 14–15)—The "veil" here represents unbelief. Paul's point was that just as the old covenant was obscure to the people of Moses' day, it was still obscure to those who trusted in it as a means of salvation in Paul's day.

the veil is taken away in Christ (v. 14)—Without Christ the Old Testament is unintelligible. But when a person comes to Christ, the veil is lifted and his spiritual perception is no longer impaired.

17 Now the Lord is the Spirit; and where the Spirit of the Lord is, there is liberty.

18 But we all, with unveiled face, beholding as in a mirror the glory of the Lord, are being transformed into the same image from glory to glory, just as by the Spirit of the Lord.

the Lord is the Spirit (v. 17)—Yahweh of the Old Testament is the same Lord who is saving people in the new covenant through the agency of the Holy Spirit. The same God is the minister of both the old and new covenants.

we all (v. 18)—not just Moses, or prophets, apostles, and preachers, but all believers

with unveiled face (v. 18)—Believers in the new covenant have nothing obstructing their vision of Christ and His glory as revealed in the Scripture.

beholding as in a mirror (v. 18)—Mirrors in Paul's day were polished metal and thus offered a far-from-perfect reflection. Though the vision is unobstructed and intimate, believers do not see a perfect representation of God's glory now, but will one day (see 1 Cor. 13:12).

into the same image (v. 18)—As they gaze at the glory of the Lord, believers are continually being transformed into Christlikeness.

from glory to glory (v. 18)—This verse describes progressive sanctification. The more believers grow in their knowledge of Christ, the more He is revealed in their lives (see Phil. 3:12–14).

1) Paul used imagery that would have been understood by most people living in the Roman Empire (2:14–16). What does this picture suggest? How does this relate to Christians and Christ?

_____

_____

_____

_____

_____

2) How did Paul contrast his ministry with the activities of the false teachers?

_____

_____

_____

_____

_____

3) What do you learn about the ancient custom of teachers presenting letters of commendation? Why were they needed?

_____

_____

_____

_____

4) Paul declares himself and Timothy ministers of the "new covenant." How does he describe this new covenant ministry? How does it differ from the "old covenant" (3:14) ministry of Moses (3:7)?

_____

_____

_____

_____

_____

5) List the things that are true of those who are under the new covenant.

_____

_____

_____

_____

GOING DEEPER

Deepen your understanding of the new covenant by reading and reflecting on Hebrews 8.

1   *Now this is the main point of the things we are saying: We have such a High Priest, who is seated at the right hand of the throne of the Majesty in the heavens,*

2   *a Minister of the sanctuary and of the true tabernacle which the Lord erected, and not man.*

3   *For every high priest is appointed to offer both gifts and sacrifices. Therefore it is necessary that this One also have something to offer.*

4   *For if He were on earth, He would not be a priest, since there are priests who offer the gifts according to the law;*

5   who serve the copy and shadow of the heavenly things, as Moses was divinely instructed when he was about to make the tabernacle. For He said, "See that you make all things according to the pattern shown you on the mountain."

6   But now He has obtained a more excellent ministry, inasmuch as He is also Mediator of a better covenant, which was established on better promises.

7   For if that first covenant had been faultless, then no place would have been sought for a second.

8   Because finding fault with them, He says: "Behold, the days are coming, says the LORD, when I will make a new covenant with the house of Israel and with the house of Judah—

9   not according to the covenant that I made with their fathers in the day when I took them by the hand to lead them out of the land of Egypt; because they did not continue in My covenant, and I disregarded them, says the LORD.

10   For this is the covenant that I will make with the house of Israel after those days, says the LORD: I will put My laws in their mind and write them on their hearts; and I will be their God, and they shall be My people.

11   None of them shall teach his neighbor, and none his brother, saying, 'Know the LORD,' for all shall know Me, from the least of them to the greatest of them.

12   For I will be merciful to their unrighteousness, and their sins and their lawless deeds I will remember no more."

13   In that He says, "A new covenant," He has made the first obsolete. Now what is becoming obsolete and growing old is ready to vanish away.

EXPLORING THE MEANING

6) Describe the wonderful characteristics of the new covenant described in Hebrews 8.

_____

_____

_____

_____

_____

_____

7) What does Paul mean when he says, "the letter kills, but the Spirit gives life" (3:6)?

_____

_____

_____

_____

8) What "veils" does Paul speak about? How does he use this term?

_____

_____

_____

9) What does 3:18 suggest about our calling and destiny as believers?

_____

_____

_____

_____

Truth for Today

The reflected glory in Moses' face, fading as it was (see 2 Cor. 3:7–11), symbolized the impermanence of the old covenant. Like the glory on Moses' face, the old covenant was never intended to be permanent. Its glory was a fading, passing glory. It was not the solution to the plight of sinners, since it could not save them. The old covenant prescribed what men were to do but could not enable them to do it. It provided a basis for damnation, but not salvation; for condemnation, but not for justification; for moral culpability, but not for moral purity. On the other hand, the new covenant is permanent and will never be superseded or supplemented. So comprehensive and final was Christ's death that it paid the price for the sins of the old covenant saints. Nothing may be added to His completed work. Any attempt to return to the external ritual and ceremony of the old covenant brings not a blessing, but a curse.

Reflecting on the Text

10) What are some specific ways Christians often fall back into "old covenant" ways of thinking and living?

_____

_____

_____

_____

_____

_____

_____

11) What would it look like to spread the fragrance of Christ in your sphere of influence?

_____

_____

_____

_____

_____

_____

12) Considering all that this passage says about the Spirit of God, how specifically do you need to yield to God today and walk in the Spirit?

_____

_____

_____

_____

_____

PERSONAL RESPONSE

Write out additional reflections, questions you may have, or a prayer.

_____

_____

_____

_____

_____

_____

_____

_____

_____

_____

_____

_____

_____

_____

_____

_____

_____

_____

_____

_____

_____

_____

_____

_____

_____

—4—
TRIALS OF THE MINISTRY

DRAWING NEAR

Someone has remarked, "Be more concerned about your character than your reputation. Your reputation is merely what others think you are, whereas your character is what you *really* are." Is this good counsel or not? Why? What do you think Paul would say about this?

_____

_____

_____

How does remembering the future promise of heaven and eternal reward help you endure tough times here and now?

_____

_____

_____

_____

_____

THE CONTEXT

Let's review: When Paul wrote this letter, his reputation was taking a severe beating in Corinth. A group of self-appointed apostles had infiltrated the church there, intent on ruining Paul's ministry so they could step in and control the church with their wrong ideas. They launched a fierce assault on the apostle's character and ministry. We can learn a lot from Paul's response to this baseless attack. First, he focused on the glory of Christ. Second, rather than denying the charges that he was weak and imperfect, he embraced them, declaring that the priceless truth of the gospel can flourish and shine only in humble containers. Third, he emphasized three keys to spiritual endurance: valuing spiritual strength over physical strength, valuing the future over the present, and valuing eternal realities over temporal ones.

Keys to the Text

Earthen Vessels: The vessels Paul describes here were just common pots: cheap, breakable, easily replaceable, and virtually valueless. Occasionally they were used to hide valuables, such as gold, silver, and jewelry, but most frequently they were used for ignoble, everyday purposes. Such clay pots had no intrinsic value; their only worth came from the valuables they contained or the service they performed.

Unleashing the Text

Read 4:1–18, noting the key words and definitions next to the passage.

2 Corinthians 4:1–18 (NKJV)

this ministry (v. 1)—the new covenant gospel of Jesus Christ

lose heart (v. 1)—This strong Greek term refers to abandoning oneself to cowardly surrender. Since God had called him to proclaim the new covenant, Paul could not abandon his noble calling.

we have renounced the hidden things of shame (v. 2)—"Renounced" means "to turn away from" or "to repent," and "shame" means "ugly" or "disgraceful." The phrase "hidden things of shame" refers to secret immoralities, hypocrisies, and the sins hidden deep in the darkness of one's life.

handling . . . deceitfully (v. 2)—This Greek word means "to tamper with" and was used in nonbiblical sources to speak of the dishonest business practice of diluting wine with water.

1 *Therefore, since we have this ministry, as we have received mercy, we do not lose heart.*

2 *But we have renounced the hidden things of shame, not walking in craftiness nor handling the word of God deceitfully, but by manifestation of the truth commending ourselves to every man's conscience in the sight of God.*

3 *But even if our gospel is veiled, it is veiled to those who are perishing,*

4 *whose minds the god of this age has blinded, who do not believe, lest the light of the gospel of the glory of Christ, who is the image of God, should shine on them.*

5 *For we do not preach ourselves, but Christ Jesus the Lord, and ourselves your bondservants for Jesus' sake.*

if our gospel is veiled . . . to those who are perishing (v. 3)—Paul showed that the problem was not with the message or the messenger, but with the hearers headed for hell.

the god of this age (v. 4)—Satan

this age (v. 4)—The current world mind-set expressed by the ideals, opinions, goals, hopes, and views of the majority of people. It encompasses the world's philosophies, education, and commerce.

has blinded (v. 4)—Satan blinds men to God's truth through the world system he has created. Without a godly influence, man left to himself will follow that system. Ultimately, it is God who allows such blindness (John 12:40).

image of God (v. 4)—Jesus Christ is the exact representation of God Himself

we do not preach ourselves (v. 4)—The false teachers accused Paul of preaching for his own benefit, yet they were the ones guilty of doing so.

6 *For it is the God who commanded light to shine out of darkness, who has shone in our hearts to give the light of the knowledge of the glory of God in the face of Jesus Christ.*

7 *But we have this treasure in earthen vessels, that the excellence of the power may be of God and not of us.*

8 *We are hard-pressed on every side, yet not crushed; we are perplexed, but not in despair;*

9 *persecuted, but not forsaken; struck down, but not destroyed—*

10 *always carrying about in the body the dying of the Lord Jesus, that the life of Jesus also may be manifested in our body.*

11 *For we who live are always delivered to death for Jesus' sake, that the life of Jesus also may be manifested in our mortal flesh.*

12 *So then death is working in us, but life in you.*

13 *And since we have the same spirit of faith, according to what is written, "I believed and therefore I spoke," we also believe and therefore speak,*

14 *knowing that He who raised up the Lord Jesus will also raise us up with Jesus, and will present us with you.*

15 *For all things are for your sakes, that grace, having spread through the many, may cause thanksgiving to abound to the glory of God.*

16 *Therefore we do not lose heart. Even though our outward man is perishing, yet the inward man is being renewed day by day.*

the light of the knowledge of the glory of God (v. 6)—The God who created physical light in the universe is the same God who must create supernatural light in the soul and usher believers from the kingdom of darkness to His kingdom of light (Col. 1:13).

excellence of the power may be of God and not of us (v. 7)—By using frail and expendable people, God makes it clear that salvation is the result of His power and not any power His messengers could generate (see 2:16).

always carrying about in the body the dying of the Lord Jesus (v. 10)—The suffering Paul experienced was endless.

that the life of Jesus also may be manifested in our body (v. 10)—Through Paul's weakness, Christ was put on display; Paul affirmed that his suffering was the badge of his loyalty to Christ and the source of his power.

delivered to death (v. 11)—refers to the transferring of a prisoner to the executioner

spirit of faith (v. 13)—the attitude of faith, not the Holy Spirit

I believed and therefore I spoke (v. 13)—a quotation from the Septuagint, an ancient translation of the Old Testament into Greek, of Psalm 116:10

our outward man is perishing (v. 16)—The physical body is in the process of decay and will eventually die.

inward man (v. 16)—the believer's soul, i.e., the new creation—the eternal part of the believer

being renewed (v. 16)—The growth and maturing process of the believer is constantly occurring. While the physical body is decaying, the inner self of the believer continues to grow and mature into Christlikeness (see Eph. 3:16–20).

our light affliction ... for a moment (v. 17)—The Greek word for "light" means "a weightless trifle" and "affliction" refers to intense pressure. Paul viewed the sufferings and persecutions of his life as weightless and lasting for only a brief moment.

eternal weight of glory (v. 17)—The Greek word for "weight" refers to a heavy mass. For Paul, the future glory he would experience with the Lord far outweighed any suffering he experienced in this world.

things which are seen . . . not seen (v. 18)—Endurance is based on one's ability to look beyond the physical to the spiritual; beyond the present to the future, and beyond the visible to the invisible.

17 *For our light affliction, which is but for a moment, is working for us a far more exceeding and eternal weight of glory,*

18 *while we do not look at the things which are seen, but at the things which are not seen. For the things which are seen are temporary, but the things which are not seen are eternal.*

1) In spite of many difficulties and obstacles, Paul refused to lose heart. Instead of giving in to discouragement, what did he do?

_____

_____

_____

_____

2) What facts about Satan are revealed in this passage?

_____

_____

_____

_____

3) How does Paul describe his ministry? What words does he use?

_____

_____

_____

_____

_____

4) What encouraging expressions of faith and hope do you see in
2 Corinthians 4?

_____

_____

_____

_____

5) Paul concludes this passage with an interesting paragraph about suffering
(vv. 16–18). What is his unique perspective? How does he compare
temporal hardships with eternal glory?

_____

_____

_____

_____

_____

GOING DEEPER

Read more about how Paul handled hard times in 2 Corinthians 11:23–33.

23 *Are they ministers of Christ?—I speak as a fool—I am more: in labors
more abundant, in stripes above measure, in prisons more frequently, in
deaths often.*

24 *From the Jews five times I received forty stripes minus one.*

25 *Three times I was beaten with rods; once I was stoned; three times I was
shipwrecked; a night and a day I have been in the deep;*

26 *in journeys often, in perils of waters, in perils of robbers, in perils of my
own countrymen, in perils of the Gentiles, in perils in the city, in perils in
the wilderness, in perils in the sea, in perils among false brethren;*

27 *in weariness and toil, in sleeplessness often, in hunger and thirst, in
fastings often, in cold and nakedness—*

28 *besides the other things, what comes upon me daily: my deep concern for
all the churches.*

29 *Who is weak, and I am not weak? Who is made to stumble, and I do not
burn with indignation?*

30 *If I must boast, I will boast in the things which concern my infirmity.*

31 *The God and Father of our Lord Jesus Christ, who is blessed forever, knows that I am not lying.*

32 *In Damascus the governor, under Aretas the king, was guarding the city of the Damascenes with a garrison, desiring to arrest me;*

33 *but I was let down in a basket through a window in the wall, and escaped from his hands.*

EXPLORING THE MEANING

6) Why does Paul speak so much in this passage about his assorted struggles and trials? Is he complaining? Bragging?

_____

_____

_____

_____

_____

7) What does Paul mean when he says, "we have this treasure in earthen vessels" (2 Cor. 4:7)? What treasure?

_____

_____

_____

_____

_____

8) What is the significance of the multiple references to "glory" in this chapter?

_____

_____

_____

_____

_____

9) How does keeping an eternal perspective provide Christians with endurance, hope, and joy?

_____

_____

_____

_____

_____

_____

TRUTH FOR TODAY

How do believers experience triumph in the midst of trouble? How do they appropriate God's promised help in tribulation? By gazing at the glory of God revealed in the face of Jesus Christ in the mirror of Scripture. Nowhere is God's glory more clearly manifest than in the Person of His Son. Therefore, the only way to successfully live the Christian life is by "beholding . . . the glory of the Lord" (3:18 NKJV) or by "looking unto Jesus, the author and finisher of our faith, who for the joy that was set before Him endured the cross, despising the shame, and has sat down at the right hand of the throne of God" (Heb. 12:2 NKJV).

REFLECTING ON THE TEXT

10) List some practical ways a Christian can develop the habit of "beholding the glory of the Lord." How does one do that while working, driving, cleaning house, etc.?

_____

_____

_____

_____

_____

_____

11) List three specific ways you can manifest (or reveal) the life of Jesus in your "earthen vessel" today.

_____

_____

_____

_____

_____

PERSONAL RESPONSE

Write out additional reflections, questions you may have, or a prayer.

_____

_____

_____

_____

_____

_____

_____

_____

_____

_____

_____

_____

_____

_____

_____

_____

THE MESSAGE OF THE MINISTRY

DRAWING NEAR

Think back on any ministry experiences you've had (for example, teaching Sunday school, leading a small group Bible study, serving as a youth group volunteer, doing inner-city outreach). What have been your ministry highlights and "lowlights"?

_____

_____

_____

_____

_____

What images come to mind when you hear the word *heaven*?

_____

_____

_____

_____

THE CONTEXT

Paul gladly suffered in this world if it meant his gaining a reward in the world to come. And rather than fearing death, the tireless apostle actually longed for heaven. In 2 Corinthians 5, Paul shared his one great consuming passion in life—to please the Lord. His daily God-centered, God-honoring activities were all motivated by the sobering reality of the judgment seat of Christ. Paul defended his ministry and integrity against the baseless lies being spread about him by the false teachers. Though such a response might leave him open to charges of pride, Paul understood that his effectiveness as an authoritative messenger of divine truth hung in the balance. Paul concluded this section of his epistle with a comprehensive theological statement about reconciliation. God offers friendship to repentant sinners through the cross of Christ. It's impossible to study these verses and not be challenged and changed!

KEYS TO THE TEXT

Judgment Seat of Christ: The "judgment seat" before which all believers will one day stand is the Greek *bēma*, a tribunal. The judgment at that place and that time will not be to dispense condemnation for sin but reward for good works, and it involves only believers. Because we stand in Christ, we will never be condemned for our sins. But we will be judged for our deeds, whether "good or bad." The word for *bad* comes from *phaulos*, meaning those mundane things that inherently are neither of eternal value or sinful, such as taking a walk, going shopping, taking a drive in the country, pursuing an advanced degree, moving up the corporate ladder, painting pictures, or writing poetry. These morally neutral things will be judged when believers stand before the judgment seat of Christ. If they were done with a motive to glorify God, they will be considered good. If they were pursued for selfish interests, they will be considered bad.

Reconciliation: The Greek word used for "reconcile" means "to change" or "exchange." Its New Testament usage refers to a change in the sinner's relationship to God. Man is reconciled to God when God restores man to a right relationship with Him through Jesus Christ. Every person who trusts in Christ alone for salvation is brought into spiritual union and intimacy with God. The atoning work accomplished by Christ's death on the cross washes away the penalty of sin and ultimately even its presence.

UNLEASHING THE TEXT

Read 5:1–21, noting the key words and definitions next to the passage.

2 Corinthians 5:1–21 (NKJV)

earthly house . . . tent (v. 1)—Paul's metaphor for the physical body (see 2 Pet. 1:13–14)

a building from God (v. 1)—Paul's metaphor for the believer's resurrected, glorified body (see 1 Cor. 15:35–50). "Building" implies solidity, security, certainty, and permanence, as opposed to the frail, temporary, uncertain nature of a tent.

1 *For we know that if our earthly house, this tent, is destroyed, we have a building from God, a house not made with hands, eternal in the heavens.*

2 *For in this we groan, earnestly desiring to be clothed with our habitation which is from heaven,*

3 *if indeed, having been clothed, we shall not be found naked.*

a house . . . in the heavens (v. 1)—A heavenly, eternal body. Paul wanted a new body that would forever perfectly express his transformed nature.

we groan (v. 2)—Paul had a passionate longing to be free from his earthly body and all the accompanying sins, frustrations, and weaknesses that were so relentless.

we shall not be found naked (v. 3)—Paul clarified the fact that the believer's hope for the next life is not a disembodied spiritual life, but a real, eternal, resurrection body.

4 For we who are in this tent groan, being burdened, not because we want to be unclothed, but further clothed, that mortality may be swallowed up by life.

5 Now He who has prepared us for this very thing is God, who also has given us the Spirit as a guarantee.

6 So we are always confident, knowing that while we are at home in the body we are absent from the Lord.

7 For we walk by faith, not by sight.

8 We are confident, yes, well pleased rather to be absent from the body and to be present with the Lord.

9 Therefore we make it our aim, whether present or absent, to be well pleasing to Him.

10 For we must all appear before the judgment seat of Christ, that each one may receive the things done in the body, according to what he has done, whether good or bad.

11 Knowing, therefore, the terror of the Lord, we persuade men; but we are well known to God, and I also trust are well known in your consciences.

12 For we do not commend ourselves again to you, but give you opportunity to boast on our behalf, that you may have an answer for those who boast in appearance and not in heart.

mortality . . . swallowed up by life (v. 4)—Paul wanted the fullness of all that God had planned for him in eternal life, when all that is earthly and human will cease to be.

for this very thing (v. 5)—more precisely translated "purpose"

at home in the body . . . absent from the Lord (v. 6)—While a believer is alive on earth, he is away from the fullness of God's presence.

absent from the body . . . present with the Lord (v. 8)—Because heaven is a better place than earth, Paul would rather have been there with God.

we make it our aim (v. 9)—This does not denote the kind of proud, selfish desire that "ambition" expresses in English. "Aim" is from the Greek word that means "to love what is honorable."

whether present or absent (v. 9)—Paul's ambition was not altered by his state of being. Whether in heaven or on earth, he cared how he lived for the Lord.

well pleasing to Him (v. 9)—Paul's highest goal (see 1 Cor. 4:1–5), and ideally that of every believer

the judgment seat of Christ (v. 10)—"Judgment seat" metaphorically refers to the place where the Lord will sit to evaluate believers' lives for the purpose of giving them eternal rewards.

the things done in the body (v. 10)—This refers to actions that happened during the believer's time of earthly ministry. This does not include sins, since their judgment took place at the cross (Eph. 1:7).

whether good or bad (v. 10)—These Greek terms do not refer to moral good and moral evil. Matters of sin have been completely dealt with by the death of the Savior. Rather, Paul was comparing worthwhile, eternally valuable activities with useless ones.

the terror of the Lord (v. 11)—more clearly rendered "the fear of the Lord," referring to worshipful reverence for God

we persuade men (v. 11)—The Greek word for "persuade" means to seek someone's favor, as in getting the other person to see you in a certain favorable or desired way (see Gal. 1:10).

boast in appearance (v. 12)—Those who have no integrity, such as Paul's opponents at Corinth, have to take pride in externals, which can be any false doctrine accompanied by showy hypocrisy.

beside ourselves (v. 13)—usually means to be insane, or out of one's mind, but here Paul uses the expression to describe himself as one dogmatically devoted to truth

the love of Christ (v. 14)—Christ's loving, substitutionary death motivated Paul's service for Him.

One died for all (v. 14)—This expresses the truth of Christ's substitutionary death. The preposition "for" indicates He died "in behalf of" or "in the place of" all.

then all died (v. 14)—This statement logically completes the meaning of the preceding phrase, in effect saying, "Christ died for all who died in Him," or, "One died for all, therefore all died."

according to the flesh (v. 16)—Paul no longer evaluated people according to external, human, worldly standards (see 10:3).

13 *For if we are beside ourselves, it is for God; or if we are of sound mind, it is for you.*

14 *For the love of Christ compels us, because we judge thus: that if One died for all, then all died;*

15 *and He died for all, that those who live should live no longer for themselves, but for Him who died for them and rose again.*

16 *Therefore, from now on, we regard no one according to the flesh. Even though we have known Christ according to the flesh, yet now we know Him thus no longer.*

17 *Therefore, if anyone is in Christ, he is a new creation; old things have passed away; behold, all things have become new.*

18 *Now all things are of God, who has reconciled us to Himself through Jesus Christ, and has given us the ministry of reconciliation,*

19 *that is, that God was in Christ reconciling the world to Himself, not imputing their trespasses to them, and has committed to us the word of reconciliation.*

in Christ (v. 17)—These two words comprise a brief but most profound statement of the inexhaustible significance of the believer's redemption.

new creation (v. 17)—This describes something that is created at a qualitatively new level of excellence. It refers to regeneration or the new birth.

old things have passed away (v. 17)—After a person is regenerate, old value systems, priorities, beliefs, loves, and plans are gone. Evil and sin are still present, but the believer sees them in a new perspective, and they no longer control him.

all things . . . new. (v. 17)—This newness is a continuing condition of fact. The believer's new spiritual perception of everything is a constant reality for him, and he now lives for eternity, not temporal things.

ministry of reconciliation. (v. 17)—This speaks to the reality that God wills to be reconciled with sinners (see Rom. 5:10; Eph. 4:17–24). God has called believers to proclaim the gospel of reconciliation to others (see 1 Cor. 1:17).

reconciling the world (v. 19)—God initiates the change in the sinner's status in that He brings him from a position of alienation to a state of forgiveness and right relationship with Himself. "World" suggests that the intrinsic merit of Christ's reconciling death is infinite and the offer is unlimited. However, actual atonement was made only for those who believe.

imputing (v. 19)—This may also be translated "reckoning," or "counting." God declares the repentant sinner righteous and does not count his sins against him because He covers him with the righteousness of Christ the moment he places wholehearted faith in Christ and His sacrificial death.

20 *Now then, we are ambassadors for Christ, as though God were pleading through us: we implore you on Christ's behalf, be reconciled to God.*

21 *For He made Him who knew no sin to be sin for us, that we might become the righteousness of God in Him.*

ambassadors (v. 20)—This meant older, more experienced men who served as representatives of a king from one country to another. All believers are messengers representing the King of heaven with the gospel, who plead with the people of the world to be reconciled to God, who is their rightful King.

sin for us (v. 21)—On the cross, Christ did not become a sinner (as some suggest), but remained as holy as ever. He was treated as if He were guilty of all the sins ever committed by all who would ever believe, though He committed none.

the righteousness of God (v. 21)—The righteousness that is credited to the believer's account is the righteousness of Jesus Christ, God's Son.

1) What imagery does Paul use to refer to his earthly body? Why?

_____

_____

_____

2) Paul mentions his deep longing. What was it? Compare 2 Corinthians 5:2–4 with Philippians 1:21–24. What is his main point in both of these passages?

_____

_____

_____

3) How did Paul keep going when things got tough? What realities motivated him?

_____

_____

_____

4) What is the astounding promise of 2 Corinthians 5:17?

_____

_____

_____

_____

5) According to Paul, what is every believer's "job description" (vv. 20–21)?

_____

_____

_____

GOING DEEPER

Discover more about that coming day where we shall account for our lives before the Lord. Read 1 Corinthians 3:11–15.

11 *For no other foundation can anyone lay than that which is laid, which is Jesus Christ.*

12 *Now if anyone builds on this foundation with gold, silver, precious stones, wood, hay, straw,*

13 *each one's work will become clear; for the Day will declare it, because it will be revealed by fire; and the fire will test each one's work, of what sort it is.*

14 *If anyone's work which he has built on it endures, he will receive a reward.*

15 *If anyone's work is burned, he will suffer loss; but he himself will be saved, yet so as through fire.*

EXPLORING THE MEANING

6) How does this 1 Corinthians 3 passage help you better understand what it means to "lay up treasure in heaven" and gain eternal rewards at the judgment seat of Christ?

_____

_____

_____

_____

7) How does this passage alter your views of heaven, eternity, and the afterlife?

_____

_____

_____

8) In what ways are believers in Christ "new" (2 Cor. 5:17)? What does this really mean?

_____

_____

_____

_____

9) Use a Bible dictionary (or a regular dictionary) to look up the word *reconciliation*. What does it mean? What are the implications of being reconciled to God?

_____

_____

_____

Truth for Today

Our Lord taught repeatedly that believers will receive rewards for their faithfulness—and those rewards vary from person to person. How are these rewards determined? Our *works* will be tested for this very purpose. In that day when we stand before the judgment seat of Christ, the whole "edifice" of our earthly works will be tested by the fire of God. Some impressive superstructures will be reduced to rubble because they are built only for show—not out of lasting material. Like sets on a movie lot, these "buildings" may be magnificent and *appear* genuine, even on close inspection, but the fire will test them for what they are made of, not for what they look like. All the wood, hay, and stubble will be burned away. Scripture promises, "If anyone's work which he has built on it endures, he will receive a reward" (1 Cor. 3:14 NKJV).

Reflecting on the Text

10) What are some specific things you can change about your life today to prepare for that great day of accounting at the judgment seat of Christ?

_____

_____

_____

11) How involved are you presently in the ministry of reconciliation? What overt "outreach" activities do you involve yourself in? What are some natural, personal ways you could begin to reach out to friends, neighbors, or coworkers who do not (yet!) know Christ?

_____

_____

_____

_____

_____

PERSONAL RESPONSE

Write out additional reflections, questions you may have, or a prayer.

_____

_____

_____

_____

_____

_____

_____

_____

_____

_____

_____

_____

_____

_____

_____

—6—
THE CONDUCT OF THE MINISTRY

DRAWING NEAR

Have you ever been ostracized or persecuted because of your faith? What happened?

_____

_____

_____

_____

THE CONTEXT

As the Bible says and as experience shows, those who set out to announce the good news with power and conviction cannot expect to be popular with everyone. Christ's messengers will experience both honor and dishonor, reception and rejection. Some will hear and accept God's gracious offer of reconciliation and peace; others will choose to remain enemies of God.

Paul discussed these realities even as he penned this epistle. Despite their many shortcomings, the Corinthian believers were a blessing to him. His heart was joyful because many of them had believed the gospel. Yet the Corinthian congregation also contained imposters, masquerading as Christians, who caused Paul much heartache. Nowhere is this tension between genuine faith and unbelief better expressed than in 2 Corinthians. Let's look at Paul's secrets for persevering.

KEYS TO THE TEXT

Patience: The word used here means "endurance," though no single English word can fully express its rich meaning. It encompasses bearing up under hard labor, surviving the shock of battle, and remaining steadfast in the face of death. This kind of patience is also associated with the idea of future glory; thus, it does not describe the grim acceptance of trials, but rather faith, hope, and joy in anticipation of future glory. The word might best be rendered "triumphant patience."

47

Unleashing the Text

Read 6:1–10, noting the key words and definitions next to the passage.

to receive the grace of God in vain (v. 1)—Most of the Corinthians were saved but hindered by legalistic teaching regarding sanctification. Some were not truly saved but deceived by a gospel of works being taught by the false teachers. In either case, Paul's proclamation of the gospel of grace would not have been having its desired effect, and he would have had cause for serious concern that his many months of ministry at Corinth were for nothing.

now is the day of salvation (v. 2)—There is a time in God's economy when He listens to sinners and responds to those who are repentant—and it was and is that time (see Prov. 1:20–23; Isa. 55:6; Heb. 3:7–8; 4:7). However, there will also be an end to that time (see Gen. 6:3; Prov. 1:24–33; John 9:4).

We give no offense in anything (v. 3)—The faithful ambassador of Christ does nothing to discredit his ministry, but does everything he can to protect its integrity, the gospel's integrity, and God's integrity.

2 Corinthians 6:1–10 (NKJV)

1 *We then, as workers together with Him also plead with you not to receive the grace of God in vain.*

2 *For He says: "In an acceptable time I have heard you, and in the day of salvation I have helped you." Behold, now is the accepted time; behold, now is the day of salvation.*

3 *We give no offense in anything, that our ministry may not be blamed.*

4 *But in all things we commend ourselves as ministers of God: in much patience, in tribulations, in needs, in distresses,*

5 *in stripes, in imprisonments, in tumults, in labors, in sleeplessness, in fastings;*

6 *by purity, by knowledge, by longsuffering, by kindness, by the Holy Spirit, by sincere love,*

7 *by the word of truth, by the power of God, by the armor of righteousness on the right hand and on the left,*

8 *by honor and dishonor, by evil report and good report; as deceivers, and yet true;*

9 *as unknown, and yet well known; as dying, and behold we live; as chastened, and yet not killed;*

we commend ourselves as ministers of God (v. 4)—"Commend" means "introduce," with the connotation of proving oneself. The most convincing proof is the patient endurance of character reflected in Paul's hardships (v. 5) and the nature of his ministry (vv. 6–7).

by the Holy Spirit (v. 6)—Paul lived and walked by the power of the Spirit. This was the central reason that all the other positive elements of his endurance were a reality.

by the word of truth (v. 7)—The Scriptures, the revealed Word of God (see Col. 1:5; James 1:18). During his entire ministry, Paul never operated beyond the boundaries of the direction and guidance of divine revelation.

by the power of God (v. 7)—Paul did not rely on his own strength when he ministered.

by the armor of righteousness (v. 7)—Paul did not fight Satan's kingdom with human resources, but with spiritual virtue.

the right hand . . . the left (v. 7)—Paul had both offensive tools, such as the sword of the Spirit, and defensive tools, such as the shield of faith and the helmet of salvation, at his disposal.

as unknown (v. 9)—Paul had become unknown to his former world, and well-known and well-loved by the Christian community.

10 *as sorrowful, yet always rejoicing; as poor, yet making many rich; as having nothing, and yet possessing all things.*

making many rich (v. 10)—The spiritual wealth Paul possessed and imparted did much to make his hearers spiritually wealthy (see Acts 3:6).

1) What does the term "workers together with Him" (or "God's fellow workers") suggest?

_____

_____

_____

2) What does Paul mean when he speaks of not offending? (Some translations render this "put no stumbling blocks" in anyone's path.)

_____

_____

_____

_____

3) How does Paul describe his life as a servant of God?

_____

_____

_____

4) We often observe the unpleasant aspects of ministry. But what good things or blessings does Paul mention in his snapshot of serving found in this chapter?

_____

_____

_____

_____

_____

5) In verses 9–10, Paul speaks a series of seeming contradictions. List these and summarize what he is saying.

_____

_____

_____

_____

_____

GOING DEEPER

Read about the trials of another servant of God in Jeremiah 20:1–12.

1   *Now Pashhur the son of Immer, the priest who was also chief governor in the house of the LORD, heard that Jeremiah prophesied these things.*
2   *Then Pashhur struck Jeremiah the prophet, and put him in the stocks that were in the high gate of Benjamin, which was by the house of the LORD.*
3   *And it happened on the next day that Pashhur brought Jeremiah out of the stocks. Then Jeremiah said to him, "The LORD has not called your name Pashhur, but Magor-Missabib.*
4   *For thus says the LORD: 'Behold, I will make you a terror to yourself and to all your friends; and they shall fall by the sword of their enemies, and your eyes shall see it. I will give all Judah into the hand of the king of Babylon, and he shall carry them captive to Babylon and slay them with the sword.*
5   *Moreover I will deliver all the wealth of this city, all its produce, and all its precious things; all the treasures of the kings of Judah I will give into the hand of their enemies, who will plunder them, seize them, and carry them to Babylon.*
6   *And you, Pashhur, and all who dwell in your house, shall go into captivity. You shall go to Babylon, and there you shall die, and be buried there, you and all your friends, to whom you have prophesied lies.'"*
7   *O LORD, You induced me, and I was persuaded; You are stronger than I, and have prevailed. I am in derision daily; everyone mocks me.*
8   *For when I spoke, I cried out; I shouted, "Violence and plunder!" Because the word of the LORD was made to me a reproach and a derision daily.*
9   *Then I said, "I will not make mention of Him, nor speak anymore in His name." But His word was in my heart like a burning fire shut up in my bones; I was weary of holding it back, and I could not.*

10 *For I heard many mocking: "Fear on every side!" "Report," they say, "and we will report it!" All my acquaintances watched for my stumbling, saying, "Perhaps he can be induced; then we will prevail against him, And we will take our revenge on him."*

11 *But the Lord is with me as a mighty, awesome One. Therefore my persecutors will stumble, and will not prevail. They will be greatly ashamed, for they will not prosper. Their everlasting confusion will never be forgotten.*

12 *But, O Lord of hosts, You who test the righteous, and see the mind and heart, let me see Your vengeance on them; for I have pleaded my cause before You.*

Exploring the Meaning

6) Jeremiah did exactly what God told him to do, and he was beaten and ridiculed. Why?

_____

_____

_____

7) Why is the Christian servant's conduct so important (see 2 Cor. 6:3)?

_____

_____

_____

_____

8) Since Paul was so loving and sacrificial in his service to the Corinthians, how do we explain their indifference and insensitivity to him?

_____

_____

_____

_____

9) A friend observes: "My goodness! Why did Paul have to suffer so much, so constantly? Is that going to happen to me if I decide to follow Christ?" How would you respond?

_____

_____

_____

_____

_____

Truth for Today

Some people come to church, profess Christ, and even get baptized. Yet when trouble comes into their lives, they're gone. And they may never come back. Maybe they encountered a broken relationship, the death of a loved one, or some other struggle, and the circumstances were so overpowering that they blamed God and walked away, convinced that Christianity doesn't work.

As believers, we may experience times of struggle and doubt, but our faith will never be destroyed. We cling to the Lord despite our trials because we love Him. That kind of loving perseverance results in true blessing.

Reflecting on the Text

10) How can you maintain a right perspective and a positive attitude when your attempts to serve the Lord are met with hostility or resistance?

_____

_____

_____

11) Paul mentions spiritual weapons (v. 7). What are the resources God has provided you with to live for Him and stand strong?

_____

_____

_____

_____

12) What practical principle from this study will you implement in your life today?

_____

_____

_____

_____

_____

PERSONAL RESPONSE

Write out additional reflections, questions you may have, or a prayer.

_____

_____

_____

_____

_____

_____

_____

_____

_____

_____

_____

_____

_____

_____

_____

_____

_____

ADDITIONAL NOTES

⏤ 7 ⏤
A LOVING LEADER

DRAWING NEAR

Paul confronted the Corinthians about some difficult issues. When have you had to confront a friend or loved one about a hard issue? How did you approach it?

_____

_____

_____

_____

THE CONTEXT

Heading the list of preposterous allegations against Paul was the charge that he had no real affection for the Corinthians and that he was abusive, manipulative, and dictatorial. What could Paul do other than remind the believers of his demonstrated love to them? On the basis of this track record of unconditional love, Paul exhorted the Corinthians to open their hearts to him and to separate themselves from intimate association with unbelievers. Paul poured out his broken heart, expressing his anguish over his damaged relationship with the Corinthian believers, and his unflagging desire to repair and restore that intimate friendship. We can learn much about God-honoring relationships in this study.

KEYS TO THE TEXT

Unequally Yoked Together: This is an illustration taken from Old Testament prohibitions regarding joining together of two different kinds of livestock. By this analogy, Paul taught that it is not right to join together in common spiritual enterprise with those who are not of the same nature (unbelievers). Christians are not to be bound together with non-Christians in any spiritual enterprise or relationship that would be detrimental to the Christian's testimony within the body of Christ

Perfecting Holiness: The Greek word for "perfecting" means "to finish" or "to complete." The word *holiness* refers to separation from all that would defile both the body and the mind.

UNLEASHING THE TEXT

Read 6:11–7:16, noting the key words and definitions next to the passage.

our heart is wide open (v. 11)—Literally, "our heart is enlarged" (see 1 Kings 4:29). The evidence of Paul's genuine love for the Corinthians was that no matter how some of them had mistreated him, he still loved them and had room for them in his heart (see Phil. 1:7).

Belial (v. 15)—an ancient name for Satan, the utterly worthless one

agreement . . . temple of God with idols (v. 16)—The temple of God (true Christianity) and idols (idolatrous, demonic false religions) are utterly incompatible.

you are the temple of the living God (v. 16)—Believers individually are spiritual houses (see 5:1) in which the Spirit of Christ dwells.

these promises (7:1)—This refers to the Old Testament promises that Paul quoted in 6:16–18. Scripture often encourages believers to action based on God's promises (see Rom. 12:1; 2 Pet. 1:3).

let us cleanse ourselves (v. 1)—The form of this Greek verb indicates that this is something each Christian must do in his own life.

filthiness (v. 1)—This Greek word, which appears only here in the New Testament, was used three times in the Greek Old Testament to refer to religious defilement, or unholy alliances with idols, idol feasts, temple prostitutes, sacrifices, and festivals of worship.

We have wronged no one (v. 2)—The Greek word for "wronged" means "to treat someone unjustly," "to injure someone," or "to cause someone to fall into sin." Paul could never be accused of injuring or leading any Corinthian into sin.

we have corrupted no one (v. 2)—"Corrupted" could refer to corruption by doctrine or money, but probably refers to corrupting one's morals.

2 Corinthians 6:11–7:16 (NKJV)

11 *O Corinthians! We have spoken openly to you, our heart is wide open.*

12 *You are not restricted by us, but you are restricted by your own affections.*

13 *Now in return for the same (I speak as to children), you also be open.*

14 *Do not be unequally yoked together with unbelievers. For what fellowship has righteousness with lawlessness? And what communion has light with darkness?*

15 *And what accord has Christ with Belial? Or what part has a believer with an unbeliever?*

16 *And what agreement has the temple of God with idols? For you are the temple of the living God. As God has said: "I will dwell in them and walk among them. I will be their God, and they shall be My people."*

17 *Therefore "Come out from among them and be separate, says the LORD. Do not touch what is unclean, and I will receive you."*

18 *"I will be a Father to you, and you shall be My sons and daughters, says the LORD Almighty."*

7:1 *Therefore, having these promises, beloved, let us cleanse ourselves from all filthiness of the flesh and spirit, perfecting holiness in the fear of God.*

2 *Open your hearts to us. We have wronged no one, we have corrupted no one, we have cheated no one.*

3 *I do not say this to condemn; for I have said before that you are in our hearts, to die together and to live together.*

4 *Great is my boldness of speech toward you,*
great is my boasting on your behalf. I am filled
with comfort. I am exceedingly joyful in all our
tribulation.

5 *For indeed, when we came to Macedonia, our bodies*
had no rest, but we were troubled on every side.
Outside were conflicts, inside were fears.

6 *Nevertheless God, who comforts the downcast,*
comforted us by the coming of Titus,

7 *and not only by his coming, but also by the*
consolation with which he was comforted in
you, when he told us of your earnest desire, your
mourning, your zeal for me, so that I rejoiced even
more.

8 *For even if I made you sorry with my letter, I do not*
regret it; though I did regret it. For I perceive that
the same epistle made you sorry, though only for a
while.

9 *Now I rejoice, not that you were made sorry, but*
that your sorrow led to repentance. For you were
made sorry in a godly manner, that you might
suffer loss from us in nothing.

10 *For godly sorrow produces repentance leading to*
salvation, not to be regretted; but the sorrow of the
world produces death.

11 *For observe this very thing, that you sorrowed in*
a godly manner: What diligence it produced in
you, what clearing of yourselves, what indignation,
what fear, what vehement desire, what zeal, what
vindication! In all things you proved yourselves to
be clear in this matter.

Great is my boldness (v. 4)—This can be translated "confidence." Paul was confident of God's ongoing work in their lives (see Phil. 1:6)—another proof of Paul's love for the Corinthian believers.

boasting (v. 4)—Though the term can have the negative connotation of sinful pride, it more often has the positive connotation of praise, as in 2 Corinthians 7:4. Proper boasting is done in the Lord, and Paul's boast of praise was of what the Lord was doing in the Corinthian church.

the downcast (v. 6)—This refers not to the spiritually humble, but to those who are humiliated. Such people are lowly in the economic, social, or emotional sense (see Rom. 12:16).

I made you sorry (v. 8)—This can also be translated "I caused you sorrow."

my letter (v. 8)—the severe letter that confronted the mutiny in the church at Corinth

your sorrow led to repentance (v. 9)—The letter produced a sorrow in the Corinthian believers that led them to repent of their sins. "Repentance" refers to the desire to turn from sin and restore one's relationship to God.

sorrow of the world produces death (v. 10)—Human sorrow is unsanctified remorse and has no redemptive capability. It is nothing more than the wounded pride of getting caught in a sin and having one's lusts go unfulfilled.

what clearing of yourselves (v. 11)—A desire to clear one's name of the stigma that accompanies sin. The repentant sinner restores the trust and confidence of others by making his genuine repentance known.

indignation (v. 11)—often associated with righteous indignation and holy anger. Repentance leads to anger over one's sin and displeasure at the shame it has brought on the Lord's name and His people.

fear (v. 11)—This is reverence toward God, who is the One most offended by sin.

zeal (v. 11)—This refers to loving someone or something so much that one hates anyone or anything that harms the object of this love.

to be clear in this matter (v. 11)—The Greek word for "clear" means "pure" or "holy." They demonstrated the integrity of their repentance by their purity.

12 *Therefore, although I wrote to you, I did not do it for the sake of him who had done the wrong, nor for the sake of him who suffered wrong, but that our care for you in the sight of God might appear to you.*

13 *Therefore we have been comforted in your comfort. And we rejoiced exceedingly more for the joy of Titus, because his spirit has been refreshed by you all.*

14 *For if in anything I have boasted to him about you, I am not ashamed. But as we spoke all things to you in truth, even so our boasting to Titus was found true.*

15 *And his affections are greater for you as he remembers the obedience of you all, how with fear and trembling you received him.*

16 *Therefore I rejoice that I have confidence in you in everything.*

1) Summarize Paul's message in 6:11–13. What is he urging them to do?

_____

_____

_____

_____

2) Summarize Paul's argument against being "unequally yoked" (6:14–7:1).

_____

_____

_____

_____

3) Why are we called to be "separate and holy" (6:17–7:1)?

_____

_____

_____

_____

4) In 7:2–16, what is Paul's tone? What idea is he trying to communicate?

_____

_____

_____

_____

5) What is godly sorrow, and what good purpose does it solve?

_____

_____

_____

_____

_____

GOING DEEPER

Paul was not afraid to lovingly confront the Corinthians. For wisdom about confronting others, read Proverbs 27:5–6.

5 *Open rebuke is better than love carefully concealed.*
6 *Faithful are the wounds of a friend, but the kisses of an enemy are deceitful.*

EXPLORING THE MEANING

6) What do these ancient sayings in Proverbs tell us about confrontation? How can "wounding a friend" be a good thing?

_____

_____

_____

_____

_____

7) How do we "cleanse" ourselves and "perfect holiness in the fear of God" (2 Cor. 7:1)?

_____

_____

_____

_____

_____

8) When does interaction with unbelievers (for the sake of reaching them with the gospel) cross the line and become "unequal yoking"? Can you give some specific examples of this?

_____

_____

_____

_____

9) Note the steps Paul took to mend the misunderstandings between the Corinthians and himself. What can we learn from this passage about trying to fix a damaged relationship?

_____

_____

_____

_____

_____

TRUTH FOR TODAY

What is love? How do you demonstrate it? To be able to practice love, you need to know what it is biblically. Throughout Scripture, love is characterized as an action. First of all, love teaches the truth to others and ministers to their needs (Eph. 4:15; Heb. 6:10). It sets an example by serving others and stimulating them to grow (Gal. 5:13). It covers other people's faults and forgives (Eph. 4:32; 1 Pet. 4:8). Love also endures the problems and idiosyncrasies of others and sacrifices on their behalf (John 15:13–14; 1 Cor. 13:7). Sometimes love must be tough and confrontational in order to heal and restore. Self-sacrificial love gives spiritual truth, help, and concern to those in need. We owe everyone that kind of love and should not owe anything else (Rom. 13:8). That's the heart of Christian living; it's the magnet that attracts the world.

REFLECTING ON THE TEXT

10) Do you have relationships with non-Christians that are "too close"? How, if at all, can you extricate yourself from these unhealthy entanglements? What can you do to obey the commands of 2 Corinthians 6:14–18? [Note: You may wish to schedule an appointment with your pastor to talk about this issue.]

———————————————————————

———————————————————————

———————————————————————

———————————————————————

———————————————————————

———————————————————————

11) Do you have Christian friends with whom you are at odds? What steps will you take today to restore the relationship in a way that honors God?

———————————————————————

———————————————————————

———————————————————————

———————————————————————

———————————————————————

———————————————————————

Personal Response

Write out additional reflections, questions you may have, or a prayer.

_____

_____

_____

_____

_____

_____

_____

_____

_____

_____

_____

_____

_____

_____

_____

_____

_____

_____

_____

_____

_____

_____

_____

_____

_____

_____

8

GIVING

DRAWING NEAR

Who is the most generous person you know? Is that person wealthy or not so wealthy?

_____

_____

_____

_____

What goes through your mind when your preacher speaks on tithing and giving?

_____

_____

_____

_____

_____

THE CONTEXT

When, how, and why should Christians give? These questions are answered in this lesson, the most detailed model of Christian giving in the New Testament. Paul discusses _patterns_ of giving, citing first the generosity of the Macedonians and then the ultimate example of sacrifice, Jesus Christ. Then he outlines the _purpose_, the right _procedures_, and finally the _promise_ of giving. Done in the right spirit, giving is the path to true, ultimate prosperity.

Paul's immediate desire was to motivate the Christians at Corinth to complete a collection for the needy believers in the Jerusalem church. Through his inspired words, God wants to remind us that we will "reap" according to how generously we "sow." Realize that God doesn't promise to reward generous givers so they can consume these additional blessings on their own desires. On the contrary, this spiritual law of "sowing and reaping" is meant to further the kingdom of God. It's in submission to that process that we find a joy that transcends any and all forms of worldly happiness.

Keys to the Text

Cheerful Giver: Giving is not to be done "grudgingly," which literally means with "sorrow, grief, or pain." Christians should never give out of an attitude of remorse, regret, or reluctance, or in a spirit of mourning over parting with what is being given. The giving that God approves should be cheerful (from the Greek word *hilaros*, "hilarious"). This kind of giving comes from the heart rather than external coercion. We are to be happy, joyous givers in view of the privilege of giving.

Unleashing the Text

Read 8:1–9:15, noting the key words and definitions next to the passage.

2 Corinthians 8:1–9:15 (NKJV)

1 *Moreover, brethren, we make known to you the grace of God bestowed on the churches of Macedonia:*

2 *that in a great trial of affliction the abundance of their joy and their deep poverty abounded in the riches of their liberality.*

3 *For I bear witness that according to their ability, yes, and beyond their ability, they were freely willing,*

4 *imploring us with much urgency that we would receive the gift and the fellowship of the ministering to the saints.*

5 *And not only as we had hoped, but they first gave themselves to the Lord, and then to us by the will of God.*

6 *So we urged Titus, that as he had begun, so he would also complete this grace in you as well.*

grace of God (v. 1)—The generosity of the churches of Macedonia was motivated by God's grace.

churches of Macedonia (v. 1)—Macedonia was the northern Roman province of Greece, basically an impoverished province that had been ravaged by many wars and even then was being plundered by Roman authority and commerce.

abundance of their joy (v. 2)—"Abundance" means "surplus." In spite of their difficult circumstances, the churches' joy rose above their pain because of their devotion to the Lord and the causes of His kingdom.

deep poverty (v. 2)—"Deep" means "according to the depth," or "extremely deep." "Poverty" refers to the most severe type of economic deprivation, the kind that caused a person to become a beggar.

riches of their liberality (v. 2)—The Greek word for "liberality" can be translated "generosity" or "sincerity." It is the opposite of duplicity or being double-minded. The Macedonian believers were rich in their single-minded, selfless generosity to God and to others.

the gift and the fellowship (v. 4)—"Gift" means "grace." The Macedonian Christians implored Paul for the special grace of being able to have fellowship and be partners in supporting the poor saints in Jerusalem. They viewed giving as a privilege, not an obligation (see 9:7).

first (v. 5)—This refers not to time but priority. Of first priority to the Macedonians was to present themselves as sacrifices to God (see Rom. 12:1–2; 1 Pet. 2:5). Generous giving follows personal dedication.

7 But as you abound in everything—in faith, in speech, in knowledge, in all diligence, and in your love for us—see that you abound in this grace also.

8 I speak not by commandment, but I am testing the sincerity of your love by the diligence of others.

9 For you know the grace of our Lord Jesus Christ, that though He was rich, yet for your sakes He became poor, that you through His poverty might become rich.

10 And in this I give advice: It is to your advantage not only to be doing what you began and were desiring to do a year ago;

11 but now you also must complete the doing of it; that as there was a readiness to desire it, so there also may be a completion out of what you have.

12 For if there is first a willing mind, it is accepted according to what one has, and not according to what he does not have.

13 For I do not mean that others should be eased and you burdened;

14 but by an equality, that now at this time your abundance may supply their lack, that their abundance also may supply your lack—that there may be equality.

15 As it is written, "He who gathered much had nothing left over, and he who gathered little had no lack."

16 But thanks be to God who puts the same earnest care for you into the heart of Titus.

17 For he not only accepted the exhortation, but being more diligent, he went to you of his own accord.

18 And we have sent with him the brother whose praise is in the gospel throughout all the churches,

you abound in everything (v. 7)—The giving of the Corinthians was to be in harmony with other Christian virtues that Paul already recognized in them: "faith"—sanctifying trust in the Lord; "speech"—sound doctrine; "knowledge"—the application of doctrine; "diligence"—eagerness and spiritual passion; and "love"—the love of choice, inspired by their leaders.

not by commandment (v. 8)—Freewill giving is never according to obligation or command.

though He was rich (v. 9)—As the second Person of the Trinity, Christ is as rich as God is rich.

He became poor (v. 9)—a reference to Christ's incarnation

that you . . . might become rich (v. 9)—Believers become spiritually rich through the sacrifice and impoverishment of Christ (Phil. 2:5–8).

complete the doing of it (v. 11)—The Corinthians needed to finish what they had started by completing the collection (see Luke 9:62; 1 Cor. 16:2).

according to what one has (v. 12)—Whatever one has is the resource out of which he should give; that is why there are no set amounts or percentages for giving anywhere stated in the New Testament.

equality (v. 14)—This Greek word gives us the English word *isostasy*, which refers to a condition of equilibrium. Thus the term could also be translated "balance" or "equilibrium." The idea is that in the body of Christ, some believers who have more than they need should help those who have far less than they need (see 1 Tim. 6:17–18).

the brother (v. 18)—This man is unnamed because he was so well-known, prominent, and unimpeachable. He was a distinguished preacher, and he was able to add credibility to the enterprise of taking the collection to Jerusalem.

19 *and not only that, but who was also chosen by the churches to travel with us with this gift, which is administered by us to the glory of the Lord Himself and to show your ready mind,*

20 *avoiding this: that anyone should blame us in this lavish gift which is administered by us—*

21 *providing honorable things, not only in the sight of the Lord, but also in the sight of men.*

22 *And we have sent with them our brother whom we have often proved diligent in many things, but now much more diligent, because of the great confidence which we have in you.*

23 *If anyone inquires about Titus, he is my partner and fellow worker concerning you. Or if our brethren are inquired about, they are messengers of the churches, the glory of Christ.*

24 *Therefore show to them, and before the churches the proof of your love and of our boasting on your behalf.*

9:1 *Now concerning the ministering to the saints, it is superfluous for me to write to you;*

2 *for I know your willingness, about which I boast of you to the Macedonians, that Achaia was ready a year ago; and your zeal has stirred up the majority.*

3 *Yet I have sent the brethren, lest our boasting of you should be in vain in this respect, that, as I said, you may be ready;*

4 *lest if some Macedonians come with me and find you unprepared, we (not to mention you!) should be ashamed of this confident boasting.*

5 *Therefore I thought it necessary to exhort the brethren to go to you ahead of time, and prepare your generous gift beforehand, which you had previously promised, that it may be ready as a matter of generosity and not as a grudging obligation.*

6 *But this I say: He who sows sparingly will also reap sparingly, and he who sows bountifully will also reap bountifully.*

grudging obligation (9:5)—Denotes a grasping to get more and keep it at the expense of others. This attitude emphasizes selfishness and pride, which can have a very detrimental effect on giving.

bountifully (v. 6)—Derived from the Greek word which gives us the word *eulogy* ("blessing"). God gives a return on the amount one invests with Him. Invest a little, receive a little, and vice versa (see Luke 6:38).

7 *So let each one give as he purposes in his heart, not grudgingly or of necessity; for God loves a cheerful giver.*

8 *And God is able to make all grace abound toward you, that you, always having all sufficiency in all things, may have an abundance for every good work.*

9 *As it is written: "He has dispersed abroad, He has given to the poor; His righteousness endures forever."*

10 *Now may He who supplies seed to the sower, and bread for food, supply and multiply the seed you have sown and increase the fruits of your righteousness,*

11 *while you are enriched in everything for all liberality, which causes thanksgiving through us to God.*

12 *For the administration of this service not only supplies the needs of the saints, but also is abounding through many thanksgivings to God,*

13 *while, through the proof of this ministry, they glorify God for the obedience of your confession to the gospel of Christ, and for your liberal sharing with them and all men,*

14 *and by their prayer for you, who long for you because of the exceeding grace of God in you.*

15 *Thanks be to God for His indescribable gift!*

as he purposes (v. 7)—The term translated "purposes" occurs only here in the New Testament and indicates a premeditated, predetermined plan of action that is done from the heart voluntarily, but not impulsively.

grudgingly (v. 7)—Literally, "with grief," "sorrow," or "sadness," which indicates an attitude of depression, regret, and reluctance that accompanies something done strictly out of a sense of duty and obligation, but not joy.

of necessity (v. 7)—"Compulsion." This refers to external pressure and coercion, quite possibly accompanied by legalism. Believers are not to give based on the demands of others, or according to any arbitrary standards or set amounts.

all grace abound toward you (v. 8)—God possesses an infinite amount of grace, and He gives it lavishly, without holding back (see 1 Chron. 29:14). Here "grace" does not refer to spiritual graces, but to money and material needs.

all sufficiency (v. 8)—In secular Greek philosophy, this was the proud contentment of self-sufficiency that supposedly led to true happiness. Paul sanctifies the secular term and says that God, not man, will supply everything needed for real happiness and contentment (see Phil. 4:19).

abundance for every good work. (v. 8)—God gives back lavishly to generous, cheerful givers, not so they may satisfy selfish, nonessential desires, but so they may meet the variety of needs others have (see Deut. 15:10–11).

administration of this service (v. 12)— "Administration," which may also be translated "service," is a priestly word from which we get *liturgy*. Paul viewed the entire collection project as a spiritual, worshipful enterprise that was primarily being offered to God to glorify Him.

proof of this ministry (v. 13)—The Jewish believers, who already doubted the validity of Gentile salvation, were especially skeptical of the Corinthians since their church had so many problems. The Corinthians' involvement in the collection would help to put those doubts to rest.

1) What surprises you about Paul's description of the Macedonians' generosity? (vv. 8:1–5) What phrases does he use? What was their situation?

_____

_____

_____

_____

2) What does Paul mean when he urges the Corinthians to "abound in this grace" of giving?

_____

_____

_____

3) In verses 8:13–15, what does Paul mean when he speaks of an "equality" in these matters of giving and receiving?

_____

_____

_____

4) Why did Paul send Titus? What financial principles do you see here (8:16–24)?

_____

_____

_____

_____

5) What is the main message conveyed in 9:6–11?

_____

_____

_____

_____

Going Deeper

Add to your biblical understanding of how to view worldly wealth by reading 1 Timothy 6:6–19.

6 *Now godliness with contentment is great gain.*

7 *For we brought nothing into this world, and it is certain we can carry nothing out.*

8 *And having food and clothing, with these we shall be content.*

9 *But those who desire to be rich fall into temptation and a snare, and into many foolish and harmful lusts which drown men in destruction and perdition.*

10 *For the love of money is a root of all kinds of evil, for which some have strayed from the faith in their greediness, and pierced themselves through with many sorrows.*

11 *But you, O man of God, flee these things and pursue righteousness, godliness, faith, love, patience, gentleness.*

12 *Fight the good fight of faith, lay hold on eternal life, to which you were also called and have confessed the good confession in the presence of many witnesses.*

13 *I urge you in the sight of God who gives life to all things, and before Christ Jesus who witnessed the good confession before Pontius Pilate,*

14 *that you keep this commandment without spot, blameless until our Lord Jesus Christ's appearing,*

15 *which He will manifest in His own time, He who is the blessed and only Potentate, the King of kings and Lord of lords,*

16 *who alone has immortality, dwelling in unapproachable light, whom no man has seen or can see, to whom be honor and everlasting power. Amen.*

17 *Command those who are rich in this present age not to be haughty, nor to trust in uncertain riches but in the living God, who gives us richly all things to enjoy.*

18 *Let them do good, that they be rich in good works, ready to give, willing to share,*

19 *storing up for themselves a good foundation for the time to come, that they may lay hold on eternal life.*

Exploring the Meaning

6) Summarize Paul's warning to Timothy. In what ways is being eager for money a "dangerous" attitude?

_____

_____

_____

7) Some preachers say, "You can't outgive God." Is this statement in line with Paul's teaching in 2 Corinthians 8–9? Why or why not?

_____

_____

_____

_____

8) What are the most common reasons Christians say they don't give? How does this passage speak to these?

_____

_____

_____

_____

Truth for Today

How people view money is an effective barometer of their spirituality. Money is neither good nor bad in itself; corrupt people can put it to evil uses, while good people can put it to righteous uses. Though it is morally neutral, what people do with their money reflects their internal morality. In the words of Jesus, "Where your treasure is, there your heart will be also" (Luke 12:34 NKJV). Significantly, the only direct quote from Jesus' earthly ministry recorded outside of the Gospels addresses the issue of giving, "It is more blessed to give than to receive" (Acts 20:35 NKJV). This promise, and many others like it in Scripture, should stimulate believers to be sacrificially generous givers.

Reflecting on the Text

9) What practical steps can you take today to evaluate and increase your financial support of the work of God?

_____

_____

_____

_____

_____

10) How does a reluctant giver become a more cheerful giver? Which are you?

_____

_____

_____

_____

_____

Personal Response

Write out additional reflections, questions you may have, or a prayer.

_____

_____

_____

_____

_____

_____

_____

ADDITIONAL NOTES

9

PAUL'S AUTHORITY

DRAWING NEAR

Paul was no stranger to hateful accusations. Have you ever been unfairly accused or misrepresented? Describe that experience.

_____

_____

_____

_____

How did it feel to have people say untrue things about you? Did you defend yourself? Why or why not?

_____

_____

_____

_____

THE CONTEXT

Many scholars wonder about the abrupt change in tone from the first nine chapters of 2 Corinthians to the final four. The best interpretation recognizes chapters 1–9 as being addressed to the silent majority struggling to follow Paul's leadership, while chapters 10–13 pertain more to the vocal minority still heavily influenced by the false teachers in the church. In truth, chapters 10–13 do form a logical conclusion to chapters 1–9, as Paul prepared the Corinthians for his promised visit.

The shift in tone can be explained this way: The issues facing the Corinthians were critical enough for Paul to set aside his characteristic humility. In light of the growing influence of false teachers in Corinth, Paul used blunt and forceful language, employed a warfare analogy, and then conducted a "short course" about how to recognize a man of God. His powerful words can help make us stronger Christians.

Keys to the Text

Strongholds: Formidable spiritual "fortresses" manned by the forces of hell can be demolished only by spiritual weapons wielded by godly believers—singularly the "sword of the Spirit" (Eph. 6:17 NKJV). The idea of a fortresses for the New Testament reader conveys the thought of a fortified, seemingly impregnable "safe" place. Corinth, like most major cities in Greece, had an acropolis. Located on a mountain near the city, this was a fortified place into which inhabitants could retreat when attacked. The word was also used in extrabiblical Greek writings to refer to a tomb or a prison. People under siege in a fortress were imprisoned there by the attacking forces. Paul used this word in a spiritual sense to express the truth that fleshly weapons cannot successfully assault the formidable strongholds in which sinners have entrenched themselves. To successfully fight the spiritual war requires weapons from the heavenly arsenal.

Unleashing the Text

Read 10:1–18, noting the key words and definitions next to the passage.

meekness (v. 1)—This is the humble and gentle attitude that expresses itself in patient endurance of unfair treatment. A meek person is not bitter or angry, and he does not seek revenge when wronged.

lowly . . . bold toward you (v. 1)—Paul sarcastically repeated another feature of the Corinthians' accusation against him; sadly, they had mistaken his gentleness and meekness toward them for weakness.

walk in the flesh (v. 3)—Paul affirmed that he did walk in the flesh in a physical sense; he was a real human being, though he possessed the power and authority of an apostle of Jesus Christ (see 4:7, 16; 5:1).

war according to the flesh (v. 3)—Although a man, Paul did not fight the spiritual battle for men's souls using human ingenuity, worldly wisdom, or clever methodologies.

our warfare (v. 4)—The motif of the Christian life as warfare is a common one in the New Testament.

carnal (v. 4)—human

arguments (v. 5)—Thoughts, ideas, speculations, reasonings, philosophies, and false religions are the ideological forts in which men barricade themselves against God and the gospel (see 1 Cor. 3:20).

2 Corinthians 10:1–18 (NKJV)

1 *Now I, Paul, myself am pleading with you by the meekness and gentleness of Christ— who in presence am lowly among you, but being absent am bold toward you.*

2 *But I beg you that when I am present I may not be bold with that confidence by which I intend to be bold against some, who think of us as if we walked according to the flesh.*

3 *For though we walk in the flesh, we do not war according to the flesh.*

4 *For the weapons of our warfare are not carnal but mighty in God for pulling down strongholds,*

5 *casting down arguments and every high thing that exalts itself against the knowledge of God, bringing*

every thought into captivity to the obedience of
Christ,

6 and being ready to punish all disobedience when
your obedience is fulfilled.

7 Do you look at things according to the outward
appearance? If anyone is convinced in himself that
he is Christ's, let him again consider this in himself,
that just as he is Christ's, even so we are Christ's.

8 For even if I should boast somewhat more about our
authority, which the Lord gave us for edification
and not for your destruction, I shall not be
ashamed—

9 lest I seem to terrify you by letters.

10 "For his letters," they say, "are weighty and powerful,
but his bodily presence is weak, and his speech
contemptible."

11 Let such a person consider this, that what we are in
word by letters when we are absent, such we will
also be in deed when we are present.

12 For we dare not class ourselves or compare
ourselves with those who commend themselves.
But they, measuring themselves by themselves, and
comparing themselves among themselves, are not
wise.

13 We, however, will not boast beyond measure, but
within the limits of the sphere which God appointed
us—a sphere which especially includes you.

14 For we are not overextending ourselves (as though
our authority did not extend to you), for it was to
you that we came with the gospel of Christ;

15 not boasting of things beyond measure, that is, in
other men's labors, but having hope, that as your
faith is increased, we shall be greatly enlarged by
you in our sphere,

every thought into captivity (v. 5)—emphasizes the total destruction of the fortresses of human and satanic wisdom and the rescuing of those inside from the damning lies that had enslaved them

look . . . outward appearance (v. 7)—The Greek verb "look" is better translated as an imperative, or command: "Look at what is obvious; face the facts; consider the evidence." Paul could call on his companions, and even Ananias, as witnesses to the reality of his Damascus Road experience; there were no witnesses to verify the false apostles' alleged encounters with the risen, glorified Christ.

terrify you by letters (v. 9)—The false apostles had accused Paul of being an abusive leader, of trying to intimidate the Corinthians in his letters. Paul's goal, however, was to bring them to repentance.

class ourselves or compare ourselves (v.12)—It is a mark of Paul's humility that he refused to compare himself with others, or engage in self-promotion. His only personal concern was what the Lord thought of him.

not boast beyond measure (v. 13)—In contrast to the proud, arrogant, boastful false apostles, Paul refused to say anything about himself or his ministry that was not true and God-given.

the limits of the sphere which God appointed us (v. 13)—Paul was content to stay within the bounds of the ministry God had given him—that of being the apostle to the Gentiles

(Rom. 1:5; 11:13; 1 Tim. 2:7; 2 Tim. 1:11). Thus, contrary to the claims of the false apostles, Paul's sphere of ministry included Corinth.

16 *to preach the gospel in the regions beyond you, and not to boast in another man's sphere of accomplishment.*

17 *But "he who glories, let him glory in the LORD."*

18 *For not he who commends himself is approved, but whom the Lord commends.*

1) How did Paul describe his own demeanor, attitude, and tone where the Corinthians were concerned?

_____

_____

_____

_____

2) What did Paul want to cast down (or demolish), and how did he plan to do this?

_____

_____

_____

_____

3) By reading 1 Corinthians 10 (and reading between the lines), what can we conclude about the false teachers' verbal attack on Paul? What were some of the charges they leveled at him?

_____

_____

_____

4) Paul resorts to some qualified boasting in this chapter. What were his "boasting guidelines"?

_____

_____

_____

5) According to Paul, what is more important than feeling good about oneself or commending oneself?

_____

_____

_____

_____

GOING DEEPER

Find out more about the reality of spiritual warfare by meditating on Ephesians 6:10–18.

10 *Finally, my brethren, be strong in the Lord and in the power of His might.*

11 *Put on the whole armor of God, that you may be able to stand against the wiles of the devil.*

12 *For we do not wrestle against flesh and blood, but against principalities, against powers, against the rulers of the darkness of this age, against spiritual hosts of wickedness in the heavenly places.*

13 *Therefore take up the whole armor of God, that you may be able to withstand in the evil day, and having done all, to stand.*

14 *Stand therefore, having girded your waist with truth, having put on the breastplate of righteousness,*

15 *and having shod your feet with the preparation of the gospel of peace;*

16 *above all, taking the shield of faith with which you will be able to quench all the fiery darts of the wicked one.*

17 *And take the helmet of salvation, and the sword of the Spirit, which is the word of God;*

18 *praying always with all prayer and supplication in the Spirit, being watchful to this end with all perseverance and supplication for all the saints.*

EXPLORING THE MEANING

6) How do these verses in Ephesians 6 add to your understanding of our enemy and his schemes?

_____

_____

_____

_____

7) What does Paul mean when he says that the Corinthians are only looking at things "according to the outward appearance"?

_____

_____

_____

_____

8) Define "boasting." Can you think of any situations in which it might be permissible for a Christian to engage in some God-honoring boasting? Is there such a thing?

_____

_____

_____

_____

9) Someone has said, "Never defend yourself. Your friends don't need it, and your enemies won't believe it anyway." Is this sound biblical advice? What would the apostle Paul think of it?

_____

_____

_____

_____

TRUTH FOR TODAY

The church today faces the same challenge that it always has: to sort out the true preachers from the deceivers. The sad story of the Corinthian church's gullibility has been repeated throughout history, as undiscerning believers have fallen for the lies of false teachers. As a result, churches, educational institutions, and denominations throughout the world have abandoned biblical truth. The Corinthians should have been able to tell the difference between true and false spiritual leaders, and so should today's church. True men of God are not showmen.

They do not intimidate people. They do not seek to promote themselves. They value truth enough not to tolerate error. They seek to imitate the meekness of Jesus Christ. They have a high view of Scripture and seek to preach the pure, unadulterated gospel. They are content to minister within the sphere in which God has placed them. They lead lives consistent with their teaching. They do not take credit for others' work. And they seek God's eternal glory, not temporal acclaim. The man "who serves Christ in these things is acceptable to God and approved by men" (Rom. 14:18 NKJV).

REFLECTING ON THE TEXT

10) What are the criteria Christians can use to tell a true man of God from a self-serving charlatan?

_____

_____

_____

_____

11) How would you delineate the difference between defending oneself and defending the truth?

_____

_____

_____

_____

12) What lesson are you taking away from this study? How will you put that lesson into practice?

_____

_____

_____

_____

_____

Personal Response

Write out additional reflections, questions you may have, or a prayer.

10

FALSE TEACHERS

DRAWING NEAR

Paul warned against teachers who were wolves in sheep's clothing. Think of a time when a leader or someone else you knew turned out to be vastly different in a negative way from what you first thought. How did you feel when you discovered it?

_____

_____

_____

_____

What is the most amazing Christian testimony of God's power and faithfulness you've ever heard?

_____

_____

_____

_____

THE CONTEXT

In these final chapters of his letter, Paul chose to deal firmly and directly with the false apostles and their unrepentant followers. He found defending himself distasteful. Yet he could not permit these false teachers to destroy his reputation and undermine his teaching. Beginning in chapter 11, Paul challenged the false apostles by reluctantly comparing himself to them. In that way the Corinthians would be able to distinguish a true messenger of God from a false one. In the process, he revealed his sufferings for the gospel.

KEYS TO THE TEXT

Untrained: Paul acknowledged his lack of training in the rhetorical skills so prized in Greek culture (2 Cor. 11:6). This term refers to an "ordinary, untrained person" and has a contemptuous ring to it. It reflects the false apostles' view that

Paul was a crude, amateurish, unrefined speaker. The apostle acknowledged that he was not interested in oratorical skills or technique but with the truth. He was not interested in theatrics or in manipulating his audience. He was a preacher of the gospel, not a professional orator. Therefore his message was the gospel, clear and simple. Paul knew that human eloquence draws people to the preacher, not to the cross. Faithful preaching, on the other hand, draws people to Christ, not the preacher.

Apostle: From the Greek word *apostolos,* which simply means "sent ones." Out of Jesus' many disciples, He selected twelve to be His apostles. These were the men who were sent by Jesus to take His message to the world. Paul also became an apostle by the appointment of the risen Christ, who encountered Paul on the road to Damascus (see Acts 9). Paul's apostleship was accompanied by a great deal of suffering; and then, to add to it, some false teachers in the Corinthian church doubted his authority. Thus in 2 Corinthians, Paul repeatedly defended the genuineness of His apostleship.

Unleashing the Text

Read 11:1–33, noting the key words and definitions next to the passage.

2 Corinthians 11:1–33 (NKJV)

a little folly (v. 1)—The Corinthians' acceptance of the false apostles' claims forced Paul to set forth his own apostolic credentials (see 12:11); that was the only way he could get them to see the truth.

I am jealous for you (v. 2)—Paul was concerned to the point of jealousy, not for his own reputation, but a godly zeal for their spiritual purity.

I have betrothed you to one husband (v. 2)—As their spiritual father, Paul portrayed the Corinthians as a daughter, whom he betrothed to Jesus Christ (at their conversion).

chaste virgin (v. 2)—Paul wanted them to be spiritually pure until the marriage day finally arrived.

he who comes (v. 4)—The false apostles came into the Corinthian church from the outside—just as Satan did into the Garden.

another Jesus . . . a different spirit . . . a different gospel (v. 4)—Despite their vicious attacks on him, Paul's quarrel with the false apostles was not personal, but doctrinal.

1 *Oh, that you would bear with me in a little folly— and indeed you do bear with me.*

2 *For I am jealous for you with godly jealousy. For I have betrothed you to one husband, that I may present you as a chaste virgin to Christ.*

3 *But I fear, lest somehow, as the serpent deceived Eve by his craftiness, so your minds may be corrupted from the simplicity that is in Christ.*

4 *For if he who comes preaches another Jesus whom we have not preached, or if you receive a different spirit which you have not received, or a different*

gospel which you have not accepted—you may well put up with it!

5 For I consider that I am not at all inferior to the most eminent apostles.

6 Even though I am untrained in speech, yet I am not in knowledge. But we have been thoroughly manifested among you in all things.

7 Did I commit sin in humbling myself that you might be exalted, because I preached the gospel of God to you free of charge?

8 I robbed other churches, taking wages from them to minister to you.

9 And when I was present with you, and in need, I was a burden to no one, for what I lacked the brethren who came from Macedonia supplied. And in everything I kept myself from being burdensome to you, and so I will keep myself.

10 As the truth of Christ is in me, no one shall stop me from this boasting in the regions of Achaia.

11 Why? Because I do not love you? God knows!

12 But what I do, I will also continue to do, that I may cut off the opportunity from those who desire an opportunity to be regarded just as we are in the things of which they boast.

13 For such are false apostles, deceitful workers, transforming themselves into apostles of Christ.

14 And no wonder! For Satan himself transforms himself into an angel of light.

15 Therefore it is no great thing if his ministers also transform themselves into ministers of righteousness, whose end will be according to their works.

16 I say again, let no one think me a fool. If otherwise, at least receive me as a fool, that I also may boast a little.

17 What I speak, I speak not according to the Lord, but as it were, foolishly, in this confidence of boasting.

18 Seeing that many boast according to the flesh, I also will boast.

the most eminent apostles (v. 5)—probably a sarcastic reference to the false apostles, based on their exalted view of themselves

I am not in knowledge (v. 6)—Whatever deficiencies Paul may have had as an orator, he had none in terms of knowledge of the gospel, which he had received directly from God (Gal. 1:12).

free of charge (v. 7)—Greek culture measured the importance of a teacher by the fee he could command. The false apostles therefore accused Paul of being a counterfeit, since he refused to charge for his services (see 1 Cor. 9:1–15).

I robbed other churches (v. 8)—*Robbed* is a very strong word, used in extrabiblical Greek to refer to pillaging. Paul, of course, did not take money from churches without their consent; his point is that the churches who supported him while he ministered in Corinth received no direct benefit from the support they gave him.

continue to do (v. 12)—That Paul refused to accept financial support from the Corinthians was a source of embarrassment to the false apostles, who eagerly sought money for their services.

let no one think me a fool (v. 16)—Since some of the Corinthians (following the false apostles' lead) were comparing Paul unfavorably to the false apostles, he decided to answer fools according to their folly (Prov. 26:5).

brings you into bondage (v. 20)—The Greek verb translated by this phrase only appears elsewhere in the New Testament in Galatians 2:4, where it speaks of the Galatians' enslavement by the Judaizers. The false apostles had robbed the Corinthians of their freedom in Christ (see Gal. 5:1).

takes from you (v. 20)—Better translated "takes advantage of you," the false apostles were attempting to catch the Corinthians like fish in a net (see Luke 5:5–6).

strikes you on the face (v. 20)—The false apostles may have physically abused the Corinthians, but the phrase is more likely used in a metaphorical sense (see 1 Cor. 9:27) to speak of the false teachers' humiliation of the Corinthians.

Are they ministers of Christ? (v. 23)—Paul had already emphatically denied that they were (v. 13); however, some of the Corinthians still believed they were. Paul accepted this belief for the sake of argument, then went on to show that his ministry was in every way superior to the false apostles' so-called "ministry."

In labors . . . in deaths often (v. 23)—A general summation of Paul's sufferings for the gospel; the next few verses give specific examples, many of which are not found in Acts. Paul was often in danger of death (Acts 9:23, 29; 14:5, 19–20; 17:5; 21:30–32).

three times I was shipwrecked (v. 25)—Paul does not refer to the shipwreck on his journey as a prisoner to Rome (Acts 27), which had not yet taken place.

19 For you put up with fools gladly, since you yourselves are wise!

20 For you put up with it if one brings you into bondage, if one devours you, if one takes from you, if one exalts himself, if one strikes you on the face.

21 To our shame I say that we were too weak for that! But in whatever anyone is bold—I speak foolishly— I am bold also.

22 Are they Hebrews? So am I. Are they Israelites? So am I. Are they the seed of Abraham? So am I.

23 Are they ministers of Christ?—I speak as a fool—I am more: in labors more abundant, in stripes above measure, in prisons more frequently, in deaths often.

24 From the Jews five times I received forty stripes minus one.

25 Three times I was beaten with rods; once I was stoned; three times I was shipwrecked; a night and a day I have been in the deep;

26 in journeys often, in perils of waters, in perils of robbers, in perils of my own countrymen, in perils of the Gentiles, in perils in the city, in perils in the wilderness, in perils in the sea, in perils among false brethren;

27 in weariness and toil, in sleeplessness often, in hunger and thirst, in fastings often, in cold and nakedness—

28 besides the other things, what comes upon me daily: my deep concern for all the churches.

29 Who is weak, and I am not weak? Who is made to stumble, and I do not burn with indignation?

30 If I must boast, I will boast in the things which concern my infirmity.

31 The God and Father of our Lord Jesus Christ, who is blessed forever, knows that I am not lying.

Paul had been on several sea voyages up to this time (see Acts 9:30; 11:25–26; 13:4, 13; 14:25–26; 16:11; 17:14–15; 18:18, 21), giving ample opportunity for the three shipwrecks to have occurred.

I will boast . . . my infirmity (v. 30)—To do so magnified God's power at work in him (see 4:7; Col. 1:29; 2 Tim. 2:20–21).

32 *In Damascus the governor, under Aretas the king,*
was guarding the city of the Damascenes with a
garrison, desiring to arrest me;
33 *but I was let down in a basket through a window in*
the wall, and escaped from his hands.

1) What prompted Paul to indulge in another round of verbal attacks on the false teachers in Corinth?

_____

_____

_____

_____

2) What sarcastic and harsh terms did Paul use to describe the false teachers?

_____

_____

3) Paul made a big deal about *not* taking money from the Corinthians (vv. 7–12). Why?

_____

_____

_____

_____

_____

4) What qualifications or credentials did Paul cite to justify his "boasting"?

_____

_____

_____

_____

5) List the hardships that Paul endured as a minister of the gospel.

_____

_____

_____

_____

_____

_____

_____

GOING DEEPER

To get an historical and accurate sense of Paul's volatile ministry, read the account in Acts 14:19–28.

19 *Then Jews from Antioch and Iconium came there; and having persuaded the multitudes, they stoned Paul and dragged him out of the city, supposing him to be dead.*

20 *However, when the disciples gathered around him, he rose up and went into the city. And the next day he departed with Barnabas to Derbe.*

21 *And when they had preached the gospel to that city and made many disciples, they returned to Lystra, Iconium, and Antioch,*

22 *strengthening the souls of the disciples, exhorting them to continue in the faith, and saying, "We must through many tribulations enter the kingdom of God."*

23 *So when they had appointed elders in every church, and prayed with fasting, they commended them to the Lord in whom they had believed.*

24 *And after they had passed through Pisidia, they came to Pamphylia.*

25 *Now when they had preached the word in Perga, they went down to Attalia.*

26 *From there they sailed to Antioch, where they had been commended to the grace of God for the work which they had completed.*

27 *Now when they had come and gathered the church together, they reported all that God had done with them, and that He had opened the door of faith to the Gentiles.*

28 *So they stayed there a long time with the disciples.*

Exploring the Meaning

6) Put yourself in Paul's sandals. Close your eyes and try to envision the scene you just read. Angry people have just hurled rocks at you, with the intent of killing you. And why? Because you have told them that Christ died for sinners, and if they will turn to Him in faith, they can enjoy eternal life. How would you feel? Would you keep going?

_____

_____

_____

_____

_____

_____

7) What do you think enabled Paul to persevere to such a radical degree?

_____

_____

_____

_____

8) Based on Paul's example and his scorching exposé of the false teachers in Corinth, what would you say are some indispensable qualities of a Christian minister? Try to identify 10 qualities from this passage.

_____

_____

_____

_____

_____

_____

_____

9) Paul expressed his concern that the Corinthians might possibly be corrupted (led astray) from "the simplicity that is in Christ" (11:3 NKJV). What are some false teachings that are popular right now among Christians that are subtly corrupting the church?

_____

_____

_____

_____

_____

_____

_____

TRUTH FOR TODAY

Three valuable principles may be distilled from Paul's contrast of himself with the false apostles. First, believers must not be taken in by smooth, clever, seemingly spiritual oratory. Such speech may mask satanic lies and deception. Many false teachers use biblical terms but invest them with a radically different meaning.

Second, believers must go beyond a teacher's words and examine his life. Religion is big business to false teachers, but those consumed with accumulating wealth and power are not true servants of Jesus Christ.

Finally, believers must avoid the temptation to make tolerance a virtue. Tolerance is the supreme virtue only to those who lack strong convictions. To discern the true from the false spiritual leaders is vital to the health of the church. To fail to exercise discernment is to open wide the door to the sheepfold and allow Satan's savage wolves to ravage God's flock.

REFLECTING ON THE TEXT

10) How does Paul's attitude in suffering inspire you?

_____

_____

_____

_____

_____

11) What practical precaution can you take this week to protect yourself
and your family from religious imposters and deceivers?

_____

_____

_____

_____

_____

12) Think of a believer you know who is currently experiencing trials
because of his or her faith. List three ways you could offer encouragement.
Now, pick one of those loving acts and commit to do it before the day is
done.

_____

_____

_____

_____

_____

PERSONAL RESPONSE

Write out additional reflections, questions you may have, or a prayer.

_____

_____

_____

_____

_____

_____

_____

_____

Additional Notes

APOSTOLIC CREDENTIALS

DRAWING NEAR

The Christian life is born and rooted in faith. In fact, apart from faith it is impossible to please God (Heb. 11:6). And yet, as Paul did, believers also have experiences with Christ that are difficult to articulate. What have been the most amazing and mysterious "spiritual experiences" in your life?

_____

_____

_____

_____

_____

_____

_____

THE CONTEXT

To some people the account of Paul's heavenly vision will seem out of place, coming right on the heels of the suffering and weakness described in lesson 10. Such a passage makes more sense when we remember the cultural context. Greeks believed that those who truly represented the gods would experience mystical visions, which some tried to induce through drunken orgies. Undoubtedly, then, the false apostles claimed revelations of their own. The Corinthians, enthralled by such amazing claims, groveled before these liars. Thus, Paul regarded it necessary to briefly relate his own genuine vision.

Next Paul set about to describe how God uses suffering in the lives of His people. No text in Scripture more powerfully unfolds God's purposes in a believer's pain than does this passage. It is a gem of rare beauty; perhaps the most emotionally charged passage Paul ever penned. In these verses Paul presents irrefutable proof that he was a genuine apostle. Unlike the false apostles lurking about Corinth and leading people astray, Paul possessed genuine qualifications and true, God-given powers.

KEYS TO THE TEXT

Thorn in the Flesh: This was sent to Paul by God in order to keep him humble (12:7). Paul's use of the word *messenger* of Satan (Greek, *angelos,* or "angel") suggests the thorn in the flesh was a demon person, not a physical illness. Of the 188 uses of the Greek word, *angelos,* in the New Testament, at least 180 are in reference to angels. This angel was from Satan, a demon afflicting Paul. Possibly the best explanation for this demon was that he was indwelling the ringleader of the Corinthian conspiracy, the leader of the false apostles. Through them he was tearing up Paul's beloved church and thus driving a painful stake through Paul.

Grace: From the Greek word *charis,* this is a magnificent, rich term that appears 155 times in the New Testament. It describes God's undeserved favor to mankind. It is a dynamic force, totally transforming believers' lives, beginning at salvation, and continuing through sanctification. Grace sets the Christian faith apart from all other religions. God is gracious, benevolent, and kind, in contrast to the gods of false religions, who are at best indifferent and need constantly to be cajoled and pleased.

UNLEASHING THE TEXT

Read 12:1–13, noting the key words and definitions next to the passage.

2 Corinthians 12:1–13 (NKJV)

visions and revelations (v. 1)— Six of Paul's visions are recorded in Acts (9:12; 16:9–10; 18:9; 22:17–18; 23:11; 27:23–24), and his letters speak of revelations he had received (see Gal. 1:12; 2:2; Eph. 3:3).

caught up to the third heaven . . . caught up into Paradise (v. 2–4)—Paul was not describing two separate visions; "the third heaven" and "Paradise" are the same place (see Revelation 2:7, which says the tree of life is in Paradise, with Revelation 22:14, which says it is in heaven). The first heaven is the earth's atmosphere (Gen. 8:2; Deut. 11:11; 1 Kings 8:35); the second is interplanetary and interstellar space (Gen. 15:5; Ps. 8:3; Isa. 13:10); and the third the abode of God (1 Kings 8:30; 2 Chron. 30:27; Ps. 123:1).

a man in Christ (v. 2)—Though Paul's reluctance to boast caused him to refer to himself in the third person, the context makes it obvious that he was speaking about himself. Relating the experience of another man would hardly have enhanced Paul's apostolic credentials. Also, Paul's thorn in the flesh afflicted him, not someone else (v. 7).

whether in . . . or . . . out of the body (vv. 2–3)—Paul was so overwhelmed by his heavenly vision that he did not know the precise details. However, whether he was caught up bodily into heaven (like Enoch in Gen. 5:24, and Elijah in 2 Kings 2:11), or his spirit was temporarily separated from his body, was not important.

1 *It is doubtless not profitable for me to boast. I will come to visions and revelations of the Lord:*

2 *I know a man in Christ who fourteen years ago—whether in the body I do not know, or whether out of the body I do not know, God knows—such a one was caught up to the third heaven.*

3 *And I know such a man—whether in the body or out of the body I do not know, God knows—*

4 *how he was caught up into Paradise and heard inexpressible words, which it is not lawful for a man to utter.*

5 *Of such a one I will boast; yet of myself I will not boast, except in my infirmities.*

6 *For though I might desire to boast, I will not be a fool; for I will speak the truth. But I refrain, lest anyone should think of me above what he sees me to be or hears from me.*

7 *And lest I should be exalted above measure by the abundance of the revelations, a thorn in the flesh was given to me, a messenger of Satan to buffet me, lest I be exalted above measure.*

8 *Concerning this thing I pleaded with the Lord three times that it might depart from me.*

9 *And He said to me, "My grace is sufficient for you, for My strength is made perfect in weakness." Therefore most gladly I will rather boast in my infirmities, that the power of Christ may rest upon me.*

10 *Therefore I take pleasure in infirmities, in reproaches, in needs, in persecutions, in distresses, for Christ's sake. For when I am weak, then I am strong.*

11 *I have become a fool in boasting; you have compelled me. For I ought to have been commended by you; for in nothing was I behind the most eminent apostles, though I am nothing.*

12 *Truly the signs of an apostle were accomplished among you with all perseverance, in signs and wonders and mighty deeds.*

13 *For what is it in which you were inferior to other churches, except that I myself was not burdensome to you? Forgive me this wrong!*

inexpressible words . . . not lawful . . . to utter (v. 4)—Because the words were for him alone, Paul was forbidden to repeat them, even if he could have expressed them coherently.

lest I be exalted above measure (v. 7)—God was allowing Satan to bring this severe trouble into the church for the purpose of humbling Paul, who, having had so many revelations—including a trip to heaven and back—would have been proud.

I pleaded . . . three times (v. 8)—Paul, longing for relief from this painful hindrance to his ministry, went to his Lord, begging Him (the use of the definite article with "Lord" shows Paul's prayer was directed to Jesus) to remove it.

My grace is sufficient for you (v. 9)—The present tense of the verb translated "is sufficient" reveals the constant availability of divine grace. God would not remove the thorn, as Paul had requested, but would continually supply him with grace to endure it (see 1 Cor. 15:10; Phil. 4:13; Col. 1:29).

the signs of an apostle (v. 12)—The purpose of miraculous signs was to authenticate the apostles as God's messengers (see Acts 2:22, 43; 4:30; 5:12; 14:3; Rom. 15:18–19; Heb. 2:3–4).

1) Despite his obvious misgivings, Paul elected to tell the Corinthians about his vision. How did he describe his experience?

_____

_____

_____

_____

2) What happened to keep Paul from becoming prideful about his experience?

_____

_____

_____

_____

3) What happened when Paul asked the Lord to change his situation?

_____

_____

_____

_____

4) Why did Paul say he could actually "take pleasure" in hard times and tough trials?

_____

_____

_____

_____

_____

_____

5) In 12:11–13, Paul sums up his defense of his apostleship. What is his "closing argument"?

_____

_____

_____

_____

GOING DEEPER

Read about Isaiah's jaw-dropping vision in Isaiah 6:1–8.

1 *In the year that King Uzziah died, I saw the Lord sitting on a throne, high and lifted up, and the train of His robe filled the temple.*

2 *Above it stood seraphim; each one had six wings: with two he covered his face, with two he covered his feet, and with two he flew.*

3 *And one cried to another and said: "Holy, holy, holy is the LORD of hosts; The whole earth is full of His glory!"*

4 *And the posts of the door were shaken by the voice of him who cried out, and the house was filled with smoke.*

5 *So I said: "Woe is me, for I am undone! Because I am a man of unclean lips, and I dwell in the midst of a people of unclean lips; for my eyes have seen the King, the LORD of hosts."*

6 *Then one of the seraphim flew to me, having in his hand a live coal which he had taken with the tongs from the altar.*

7 *And he touched my mouth with it, and said: "Behold, this has touched your lips; your iniquity is taken away, and your sin purged."*

8 *Also I heard the voice of the Lord, saying: "Whom shall I send, and who will go for Us?" Then I said, "Here am I! Send me."*

EXPLORING THE MEANING

6) In Isaiah's vision, what was revealed about God? About the prophet? What happened as a result of this divine encounter?

_____

_____

_____

_____

7) Someone has said, "Whenever you are blessed with an unusual sense of the presence or power of God, enjoy it and be grateful for it, but do not expect it, and certainly do not demand such visitations in the future." Why is this wise advice?

_____

_____

_____

_____

8) Scholars down through the centuries have speculated as to the nature of Paul's thorn in the flesh. What do you think it was, and why? What purpose did it serve?

_____

_____

_____

_____

9) Why do you think God heals certain people (or takes away their "thorns") and not others?

_____

_____

_____

_____

TRUTH FOR TODAY

Paul had lost all ability, humanly speaking, to deal with the situation at Corinth. He had visited there, sent others there, and written the Corinthian letters. But he could not completely fix the situation. He was at the point where he had to trust totally in God's will and power. It is when believers are out of answers, confidence, and strength, with nowhere else to turn but to God, that they are in a position to be most effective. No one in the kingdom of God is too weak to experience God's power, but many are too confident in their own strength. Physical suffering, mental anguish, disappointment, unfulfillment, and failure squeeze the impurities out of believers' lives, making them pure channels through which God's power can flow.

Reflecting on the Text

10) List the following in your life:

⌒ a minor pet peeve:

_____

_____

⌒ a moderate trial:

_____

_____

⌒ a crisis situation:

_____

_____

How can God use these things for His glory and your good?

_____

_____

_____

_____

_____

_____

11) What long-term struggles do you need to surrender to God today? How can you experience God's grace in the gritty times of life?

_____

_____

_____

_____

_____

_____

12) How, practically speaking, can you rely more on God's strength and power today, and less on your own?

_____

_____

_____

_____

_____

Personal Response

Write out additional reflections, questions you may have, or a prayer.

_____

_____

_____

_____

_____

_____

_____

_____

_____

_____

_____

_____

_____

_____

_____

_____

12

FINAL WARNINGS

2 Corinthians 12:14–13:14

DRAWING NEAR

If Paul were your pastor today, what words might your congregation use to describe him? (Circle all that you think would apply.)

caring	confrontational	intrusive	bossy
impatient	loving	bold	compassionate
consistent	crabby	defensive	awe-inspiring
nitpicky	passionate	overzealous	worried
gentle	other-centered	protective	paranoid
controlling	Christlike	egomaniacal	single-minded

List the people who have been the most influential in your spiritual life and have "built you up" in the faith.

_____

_____

_____

THE CONTEXT

It is important to remember that the backdrop of this study of 2 Corinthians was the assault on the church by false apostles. These wolves had preyed on the flock by savagely attacking Paul's credibility and forcing him to defend himself. In this final section Paul continued to differentiate himself from the false apostles, contrasting his correct view of the ministry with their wrong view. Paul demonstrated that we will be able to distinguish true men of God by qualities such as faithfulness, sacrifice, honesty, reverence, and an observable desire to build others up (rather than tear others down).

In closing, Paul laid out for the Corinthians a detailed pattern of what it means to mature in Christ. His words form a wonderful discussion of the essential elements of spiritual growth: repentance, discipline, right response to authority, authenticity, obedience, integrity, perfection, and affection. Ask God to teach you and change you as you read, ponder, and respond.

Keys to the Text

Test Yourselves: Paul told the Corinthians to test and examine their faith. This phrase means "to try, examine, interpret," and carries the idea of proving (2 Cor. 13:5). This is a common New Testament word that often refers to testing something for authenticity. It entails distinguishing between true and false, right and wrong, or good and bad. Sometimes the word denotes the process of distinguishing what is pleasing to the Lord (Eph. 5:10; see Rom. 12:2). In classical Greek it was used of assaying metals to determine purity and of testing coins both for the purity of their metals and for their genuineness.

Unleashing the Text

Read 12:14–13:14, noting the key words and definitions next to the passage.

2 Corinthians 12:14–13:14 (NKJV)

for the third time (v. 14)—The first was the visit recorded in Acts 18; the second was the "painful visit."

I do not seek yours, but you (v. 14)—Paul sought the Corinthians (see 6:11–13; 7:2–3), not their money.

14 *Now for the third time I am ready to come to you. And I will not be burdensome to you; for I do not seek yours, but you. For the children ought not to lay up for the parents, but the parents for the children.*

15 *And I will very gladly spend and be spent for your souls; though the more abundantly I love you, the less I am loved.*

16 *But be that as it may, I did not burden you. Nevertheless, being crafty, I caught you by cunning!*

17 *Did I take advantage of you by any of those whom I sent to you?*

18 *I urged Titus, and sent our brother with him. Did Titus take advantage of you? Did we not walk in the same spirit? Did we not walk in the same steps?*

19 *Again, do you think that we excuse ourselves to you? We speak before God in Christ. But we do all things, beloved, for your edification.*

20 *For I fear lest, when I come, I shall not find you such as I wish, and that I shall be found by you such as you do not wish; lest there be contentions, jealousies, outbursts of wrath, selfish ambitions, backbitings, whisperings, conceits, tumults;*

21 *lest, when I come again, my God will humble me among you, and I shall mourn for many who have sinned before and have not repented of the uncleanness, fornication, and lewdness which they have practiced.*

13:1 *This will be the third time I am coming to you. "By the mouth of two or three witnesses every word shall be established."*

2 *I have told you before, and foretell as if I were present the second time, and now being absent I write to those who have sinned before, and to all the rest, that if I come again I will not spare—*

3 *since you seek a proof of Christ speaking in me, who is not weak toward you, but mighty in you.*

4 *For though He was crucified in weakness, yet He lives by the power of God. For we also are weak in Him, but we shall live with Him by the power of God toward you.*

5 *Examine yourselves as to whether you are in the faith. Test yourselves. Do you not know yourselves, that Jesus Christ is in you?—unless indeed you are disqualified.*

6 *But I trust that you will know that we are not disqualified.*

7 *Now I pray to God that you do no evil, not that we should appear approved, but that you should do what is honorable, though we may seem disqualified.*

8 *For we can do nothing against the truth, but for the truth.*

9 *For we are glad when we are weak and you are strong. And this also we pray, that you may be made complete.*

10 *Therefore I write these things being absent, lest being present I should use sharpness, according to the authority which the Lord has given me for edification and not for destruction.*

11 *Finally, brethren, farewell. Become complete. Be of good comfort, be of one mind, live in peace; and the God of love and peace will be with you.*

a proof of Christ speaking in me (3:3)—Those Corinthians still seeking proof that Paul was a genuine apostle would have it when he arrived. They may have gotten more than they bargained for, however, for Paul was going to use his apostolic authority and power to deal with any sin and rebellion he found there.

who is not weak (3:3)—Christ's power was to be revealed through Paul against the sinning Corinthians (see 1 Cor. 11:30–32). By rebelling against Christ's chosen apostle (1:1), they were rebelling against Him.

disqualified (v. 5)—Literally, "not approved." Here it referred to the absence of genuine saving faith.

do what is honorable (v. 7)— Paul's deepest longing was for his spiritual children to lead godly lives (see 7:1)—even if they persisted in doubting him. Paul was even willing to appear "disqualified," as long as the Corinthians turned from their sin (see Rom. 9:3).

I write these things . . . for edification and not for destruction (v. 10)—a one-sentence summary of Paul's purpose in writing this letter

the God of love and peace will be with you (v. 11)—An encouragement to the Corinthians to carry out the exhortations in the first part of the verse. Only here in the New Testament is God called "the God of love" (see 1 John 4:8).

12 *Greet one another with a holy kiss.*

13 *All the saints greet you.*

14 *The grace of the Lord Jesus Christ, and the love of God, and the communion of the Holy Spirit be with you all. Amen.*

1) What analogy did Paul use to describe his relationship with the Corinthian believers?

_____

_____

_____

_____

2) How did Paul defuse the accusation that he and Titus were somehow "making money" from their ministry to the Corinthians?

_____

_____

_____

3) What sins was Paul afraid might be springing up among the Corinthians?

_____

_____

_____

_____

4) What kind of examination did Paul advocate in 13:5?

_____

_____

_____

_____

_____

_____

5) In his final words, Paul spoke about the power of Christ, "who is not weak toward you, but mighty in you" (13:3). What are some ways God showed His power among the Corinthians?

_____

_____

_____

_____

_____

_____

GOING DEEPER

Read and reflect on the importance of submitting to spiritual authority in Hebrews 13:7–9 and 17.

7 *Remember those who rule over you, who have spoken the word of God to you, whose faith follow, considering the outcome of their conduct.*

8 *Jesus Christ is the same yesterday, today, and forever.*

9 *Do not be carried about with various and strange doctrines. For it is good that the heart be established by grace, not with foods which have not profited those who have been occupied with them . . .*

17 *Obey those who rule over you, and be submissive, for they watch out for your souls, as those who must give account. Let them do so with joy and not with grief, for that would be unprofitable for you.*

EXPLORING THE MEANING

6) According to Hebrews, what should be our response to those who are over us in the Lord, that is, those who are our spiritual leaders?

_____

_____

_____

_____

_____

_____

7) Think back over the entire letter of 2 Corinthians. Review Paul's concerns, his pleading and rebuking, his tone, his expectations. How was Paul's practice of the Christian ministry different from the way many modern clergyman go about their shepherding task?

_____

_____

_____

_____

_____

_____

_____

_____

_____

_____

8) What was Paul's appeal in the last paragraph of his letter? Why are these appropriate words?

_____

_____

_____

_____

_____

Truth for Today

The inclusion of 2 Corinthians in the New Testament canon argues that the Corinthians responded favorably to the letter. Had it failed to achieve its purpose, the church probably would not have accepted it as Scripture. This letter, in which Paul poured out his heart to the Corinthians, achieved its goal of reconciling them to him. Like the rest of Scripture, it will infallibly achieve what God designed it to achieve. As God declared through the prophet Isaiah, "For as the rain comes down, and the snow from heaven, and do not return there, but water the earth, and make it bring forth and bud, that it may give seed to the sower and bread to the eater, so shall My word be that goes forth from My mouth; it shall not return to Me void, but it shall accomplish what I please, and it shall prosper in the thing for which I sent it" (Isa. 55:10–11 NKJV).

Reflecting on the Text

9) What person could prove to be an objective "sounding board" for you this week—to help you examine and "test" your own heart and spiritual condition?

_____

_____

_____

_____

10) What steps can you take to be a better follower of Christ and church member this week?

_____

_____

_____

_____

_____

11) Knowing what Paul went through with the church at Corinth, list three ways you could make your pastor's task of shepherding you more joyful.

_____

_____

_____

_____

_____

12) What are the dominant truths that you take with you from this study of 2 Corinthians? How do you intend to incorporate that into your life?

_____

_____

_____

_____

_____

_____

_____

Personal Response

Write out additional reflections, questions you may have, or a prayer.

_____

_____

_____

_____

_____

_____

_____

_____

_____

_____

_____

_____

_____

_____

_____

Additional Notes

ADDITIONAL NOTES

Additional Notes

Additional Notes

Additional Notes

Additional Notes

ADDITIONAL NOTES

Additional Notes

Additional Notes

ADDITIONAL NOTES

The MacArthur Bible Study Series

Revised and updated, the MacArthur Study Guide Series continues to be one of the bestselling study guide series on the market today. For small group or individual use, intriguing questions and new material take the participant deeper into God's Word.

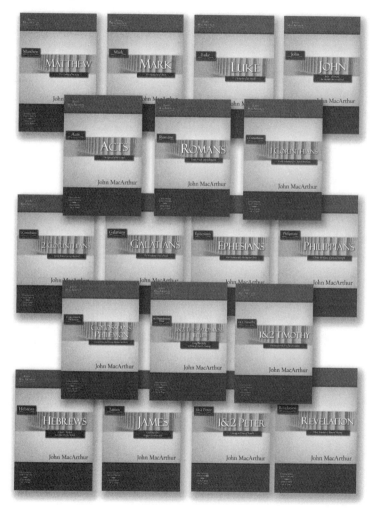

Available at your local Christian Bookstore or www.nelsonimpact.com

NELSON IMPACT
A Division of Thomas Nelson Publishers
Since 1798

www.thomasnelson.com

Look for these exciting titles
by John MacArthur

Experiencing the Passion of Christ

Experiencing the Passion of Christ Student Edition

Twelve Extraordinary Women Workbook

Twelve Ordinary Men Workbook

Welcome to the Family:
What to Expect Now That You're a Christian

What the Bible Says About Parenting:
Biblical Principles for Raising Godly Children

Hard to Believe Workbook:
The High Cost and Infinite Value of Following Jesus

The John MacArthur Study Library for PDA

The MacArthur Bible Commentary

The MacArthur Study Bible, NKJV

The MacArthur Topical Bible, NKJV

The MacArthur Bible Commentary

The MacArthur Bible Handbook

The MacArthur Bible Studies series

Available at your local Christian bookstore
or visit www.thomasnelson.com

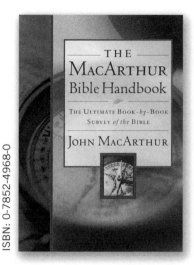
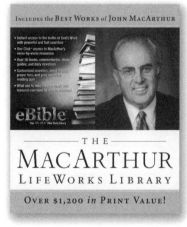

NELSON IMPACT
A Division of Thomas Nelson Publishers
Since 1798

The Nelson Impact Team is here to answer your questions and suggestions as to how we can create more resources that benefit you, your family, and your community.

Contact us at Impact@thomasnelson.com